Wielgus, Chuck.
    The in-your-face basketball book /
Chuck Wielgus, Jr. and Alexander
Wolff ; introd. by Al McGuire ;
illustrated by N.E. Wolff. -- 1st
ed. -- New York : Everest House,
c1980.
    187 p., [1] leaf of plates :
ill. ; 26 cm.
    ISBN 0-89696-067-6

    1. Basketball--United States. 2.
Playgrounds--United States. I.
Wolff, Alexander, 1957-   joint
author. II. Title.

GV885.7.W52 1980   796.32'3'0973
                                    79-25595
                                    MARC
Library of Congress
04194   512673   © THE BAKER & TAYLOR CO.   3032

The In-Your-Face Basketball Book

THE
In-Your-Face
Basketball
Book

Chuck Wielgus, Jr. and Alexander Wolff

Introduction by Al McGuire
Illustrated by N. E. Wolff

 EVEREST HOUSE   Publishers, New York

Lyrics from *At Seventeen,* by Janis Ian, reprinted by permission of Mine Music, Ltd., copyright © 1974, Mine Music Ltd. (ASCAP)

Lyrics from *Fire,* by Ohio Players, copyright © 1974, Rick's Music, Inc., used by permission. All rights reserved.

Lyrics from *Game Seven,* published by Ascent Music, Inc./Nouveau Music

Library of Congress Cataloging in Publication Data

Wielgus, Chuck.
   The in-your-face basketball book.
     1. Basketball—United States.   2. Playgrounds—United States.   I. Wolff, Alexander, 1957–   joint author. II. Title
GV 885.7.W52   1980   796.32'3'0973   79-25595
ISBN: 0-89696-067-6

Published simultaneously in Canada by
Beaverbooks, Pickering, Ontario
Manufactured in the United States of America
Designed by Joyce Cameron Weston
2 ELABII80

For our families . . .
and everyone else who appreciates the
spirit of a game that gives people of
all races, sexes, and nationalities
one more common ground.

CONTENTS

ACKNOWLEDGMENTS

WHEN we told hundreds of people around the country that we were getting up a pick-up game and wanted them to play, so many took us up on the offer that we can't possibly list them all. A blanket thanks will have to do. But the following people hit the asphalt for loose balls and deserve special mention: Carlton Alston, Steve Antrim, Lon Austin, Ed Berger, Barry Caldwell, Mike Capistran, Gary Connally, Frank Crum, Melvin Boyd Cunningham, Jon Edwards, Alec Hastings, Walter Haynes, Corinne Heyes, Rich Kelley, Dave Kindred, Suzy Laferrier, Robert Massie, Randy Melville, John Mileham, Wayne Morgan, Grace Newell, Theresa Ojibway, Rick Potter, Jim Reiman, David Remnick, Andy Rice, Robert Rodriguez, George Schauer, Frank Soule, June Steitz, Wayne Szoke, Bill Thompson, Gerry Toner, Charles Wielgus, Sr., Paul Wielgus, Stephanie Wolff, and Tony Woods.

And Bob Wright deserves separate citation for his creative critique of the manuscript and overall court sense.

INTRODUCTION

DEAN MEMINGER, a player I coached at Marquette (who later played several seasons for the New York Knicks) once said: "If you don't play ball, you can't hang out."

How true.

When you combine hanging out with basketball, you get the schoolyard brand of ball and the subculture that goes with it. I was a part of that subculture. I was never a superstar on the court, but having the ball in my hands when I was a kid made me somebody. We didn't pay much attention to weather. Our season never ended. Late in the year, the scraping of six inches of snow from the court was our warm-up. The wind off the Atlantic was like a sixth man against us (and, incidentally, against our opponent, although we never considered that). The wind always came from the East so you had to allow for it when you set up for a shot. Nobody complained. It was there and you adjusted to it.

All sorts play pick-up ball: guys and girls, blacks and whites, doctors and delinquents. They don't just play it in litter-strewn or snow-covered city schoolyards either. Everywhere—in lush suburban parks, well-paved driveways, or barnyards—the goal is that same rim, eighteen inches in diameter. And there are other goals—playing hard, shooting your best shot, and all the while enjoying it.

The schoolyard style is a far cry from that of the organized game, which weeds out the clowns, loafers, hustlers, cheaters, smoothies, wise-guys, and other hangers-on. And that colorful mix doesn't prevent the playground from producing the occasional hero, too.

What's that special thing about basketball? What has allowed the sport to develop a schizophrenic side like pick-up ball, and a nickname as affectionate as "hoop"? It's the freedom and looseness that exists inside the game's conventions.

Chuck Wielgus and Alexander Wolff have delved into the folk culture of pick-up basketball just as historians might, putting into words and pictures a part of the American jock spirit. They've described all the types you've ever run across in a gym or schoolyard: the player who does nothing but rebound and play D; the slow, fat guy who'll argue every call; the little guard who always thinks he's

My face in thine eye . . .
—John Donne

11

open; and the ego case who only runs with the very best comp. If they aren't in the text, they're between the lines. And this book touches on the feelings and thoughts that occur to any player. Don't be surprised if you find yourself smirking and saying "That's it!" to yourself while reading it.

But enough of the French pastry. Here are the numbers: the authors visited hundreds of playgrounds in states from Florida to California, contacting countless recreation people and pick-up junkies over the phone and by mail. They spent a year sifting their data. The result is included here: playground ball's first dictionary, collection of portraits of asphalt legends (many of whom no one's ever heard of), and a listing of over one hundred of the top playgrounds in the country. Like the American Express card, never leave home without it. If you're old enough to lace up your own sneakers and young enough to still remember owning a pair, you're going to love this book. That's not to say it's one of those you can't put down. On the contrary—it makes you put it down, to head for the courts to play ball and hang out.

Al McGuire

The
In-Your-Face
Basketball
Book

1. IN YOUR FACE

WHAT you *doin'*, man? You a *chump*, tha's right, you ain't nothin' but a piehead. Come on, *see* if you can pull a move on me, jes' *see*."

"Doctor" means "J," not Naismith, and the game isn't the same

You're in the midst of a friendly game of One-on-One. It's your ball and you're cautiously backing in toward the basket as your opponent toys with your psyche.

"What *is* this garbage, man? You playin' like Don Nelson, man. Like a *chump*."

Remember when it was a compliment to be told you played like Don Nelson, that poker-faced, fundamentally sound former Celtic forward?

You spin around, make a quick crossover dribble from your right hand to your left, and slip your right foot past one side of your defender. You lay the ball on the fingertips of your left hand, cock it behind your left ear, and . . .

"Chump!"

. . . float toward the basket, as he lunges for the ball like King Kong swiping at the Statue of Liberty's torch. At the last possible instant, burrowing toward the hoop, you bring the ball down to your waist and regurgitate it upward with two hands. It skids in. Now it's your turn.

"In your *face*."

You've done it—captured the magical moment that, if you're really honest, you'll admit is the object of every playground basketball encounter. If Cheech and Chong were there, they would have broken into a celebratory rendition of "Basketball Jones." And if Dr. James Naismith were there, he might well have understood, too. You see, the good Doctor was always pleased that basketball moved outdoors. He collected pictures of some of the odd places he would find descendants of the original peach basket he tacked up on the balcony of the Springfield, Mass. YMCA Training School gymnasium back in the 1890s. Within the first two decades after the game's invention, hoops made their way onto telephone poles, and into alleys and barnyards. But it's only been recently, since Dr. Naismith's death and basketball's export to all parts of the world, that the playground basketball subculture has emerged. The playground game really has everything an anthropologist would expect in a culture: its own vernacular, conventions, rituals, folk heroes, and pecking order. It even has an ideal state in that unmatchable high known as *face*.

What is *face?* The term stems from colloquial American usage, and the notions of saving face (or retaining one's self-respect) and losing it (or being utterly humiliated). Transformed into the actual acts performed on the asphalt that deal with that self-respect, *face* comes with a shot by an opponent that is so completely rejected it ends up back *in his face* or—as most know it—a successful shot taken under trying conditions, with an opponent so close that the shot could be said to be taken *in your face*.

At the root of the expression, of course, are the individual player and his ego. In the cities, where playgrounds become the spots where self-styled superstars congregate to prove their worth, making an off-balance, left-handed running hook *in your face* is like graduating from school *summa cum laude* (though your mother may not see it that way). It's too simple to say *face* is merely a matter of one-upmanship; if it were, pick-up ball wouldn't have so many devotees among casual players mainly out for exercise. What lures and holds so many is the knowledge that when they get *face*, it will be a singular moment, entirely theirs, and nothing that happens subsequently—not even an airball from inside the lane— will diminish it. It's a vicious cycle, too; once you've gotten your

LEFT:
In your face, Dr. Naismith!
(*Basketball Hall of Fame*)

RIGHT:
In your face, Idi Amin!
(*Wide World Photos*)

LEFT:
One symptom of a "basket case:" Wastebaskets stay in the far corners of rooms. (N.E. Wolff)

RIGHT:
Another symptom: You drive through the lane— exact change, that is—to the basket. (N.E. Wolff)

first fix of *face,* you're in danger of becoming a basket case. Keep an eye out for the symptoms. You'll start referring to the three major sports as baseball, football, and ball. You'll refuse to move the wastebasket in the far corner of the room closer to your desk. And it will seem as though some inexorable force is steering your car into the exact-change lanes of toll plazas.

As playground products pour into organized basketball, they bring with them elements of the playground subculture. Lloyd Free, the bombs-away guard from Brooklyn, alternately calls himself "All-World" and "The Prince of Midair." To veteran basketball people, those in the front offices and coaching profession, Free's braggadocio and everything it suggests is revolutionary. Sportswriter Roy Blount, Jr., picked up on it in a recent newspaper column when he suggested that basketball follow the lead of baseball in one respect. Baseball, it will be remembered, appends information about plays of interest—hit batsmen, for instance, or passed balls—to its box scores. Blount's idea: to indicate both the perpetrator and victim of face jobs. In baseball we see "HBP— Guidry (Burleson)"; in basketball we may soon see, in five-point type, "IYF—Free (Twardzik)." To be sure, an ominous conflict is developing in organized ball as a result of the integration of schoolyard values into the game. Listen to this anguished cry from the Pacific Northwest, from Jack Avina, coach at the University of Portland, who told *Sports Illustrated:* "It bothers me that so many modern players are involved in the facade of making a show. I hear my kids in practice talking about 'face, face.' Sometimes players are more concerned about 'face' than winning the game."

Jack Avina, you're on to something. It explains why players prefer baroque, behind-the-back passes to crisp chest passes, why they persist in shooting lay-ups without using the backboard (which is contrary to what most coaches preach), and why, even though the double pump is a "poor percentage shot," players prefer it. It has high "face-return potential" and, given the choice, today's players will take the path least traveled upon. It'll make all the difference—not necessarily in winning the game, but in making it memorable. More and more playground players are rejecting the Lombardian credo of "winning is the only thing," not because they don't care about doing well anymore, but because they've discovered that style is as important as substance. They've struck upon a middle ground that can be articulated best by paraphrasing Grantland Rice: "When the One Great Scorer comes to write upon your name, he marks not whether you won or lost, but whether you got *face* or not."

2. GOING COURTING

WHERE does the inspiration hit? In a car? Keep a pair of sneakers and a ball in the trunk and you're all set. On the sidewalk? Few playgrounders not already involved in a game turn down the requests of passersby to "shoot a few." If you simply want to play some ball, there aren't any court reservations or greens fees to worry about. Whether you feel like going half-court or running full, or merely laying the ball lazily hoopward, whether you're alone or with two others or with a full complement of players, there's a game for you.

Without being burdened with a set of cumbersome conventions, the playground has developed a game to accommodate every sort of player and every sort of style. If you're competitive and energetic, there's One-on-One; if you prefer movement and team play to showmanship, try half-court Three-on-Three. If you've developed an automatic set shot, challenge that guy who's a head taller than you and always whups you in One-on-One to a game of Around the World. On the other hand, if you shoot bricks from outside the lane but have an array of spin and bank shots in your repertoire, stick with H-O-R-S-E.

The many different types of games for one basket evolved out of necessity. Space became rarer as outdoor basketball's popularity boomed; consequently half-court ball developed. The rite of "taking it around" approximates the transition between offense and defense of a full-court game. And without court reservations, something had to be done for those awkward times when an odd number of eager players populate the pavement. The result: Games like Twenty-one and Knock-out. Here's a look at a selection of games, from *solo* to *tutti* at one basket, to straight, full-court Five-on-Five, to the shooting games for when your energies are spent.

Playing by Yourself

On a playground, in a driveway, or in a cavernous gym, you can create almost anything with just yourself, a ball, and a hoop. You're the offense, you control the defense, and if you act out small scenarios, as just about everyone does—"Down by one, three

Games to play, from One-on-None 'til when day's done

seconds left, he fakes right, spins left, and lets go a twenty-foot fallaway that's *good!*"—you'll always end up being the star of the game.

Your most obvious head fake is enough to leave your opponent groping for his jockstrap. Your twenty-footers swish through even though one defender has his hand in your face, another is tugging at your jersey, and the ref is blind. Your DeGregorian dribbling leaves defenders in its wake, even though you drop your head every time you send the ball between your legs. If your "buzzer shot" doesn't happen to drop, you can use your imagination to give yourself a few more chances: A phantom ref can blow his imaginary whistle, sending you to the foul line with no time left and a chance to win it. "All he has to do is sink both ends of this one-and-one!" (As many sportscasters as ballplayers get their starts playing by themselves on near-empty courts.) If you miss the one-and-one, the opposing coach was assessed a technical for throwing a towel, and you've been granted a reprieve.

If One-on-None gets to be a bit jading in its one-sidedness, there's a game that can make it more interesting. It's similar to those re-created sports board games. You become every player for both teams. If you hit your first shot, from anywhere on the court, team "A" gets two points. If you miss, but net your follow-up, "A" registers one. Then possession switches to team "B" and the same rules apply. You play to twenty-five—all the while keeping the images of scoreboard lights, ecstatic fans, and befuddled defenders in mind.

The opportunity to play by yourself is a luxury. In the city, where space is at a premium, courts tend to be used to their capacity. Players don't have the opportunity to perfect their shooting with shot after shot, so their strengths are usually the drive and shot in traffic, which have been developed through competition. But in the suburbs, and especially in rural areas, it's solo repetition that promises success. The parabolic path of ex-UCLA forward Lynn Shackleford's jump shots out of the corners was a suburban trait, the result of practicing in his driveway, which had telephone wires running over it. In Missouri, Bill Bradley used to position chairs in his driveway to indicate defenders, and he would dribble in and out of them while wearing cardboard blinders designed to improve his peripheral vision. Jimmy "The Human" Rayl, the Big Ten's all-time leading scorer, learned the game on the second floor of a barn in Kokomo, Indiana. Those watching Rayl play in college swore they could re-create the structure of that barn simply by watching the pattern of his shots from different spots on the floor.

OPPOSITE PAGE:
On a playground you can create almost anything with yourself, a ball, and a hoop.

Connie Hawkins, one-on-none. (John Launois, Black Star)

And Don Nelson, who grew up in Iowa, had a unique incentive to make his corner shots as he was growing up: If he missed long, the ball would end up in a pile of chicken evidence.

For anyone playing alone, there's nothing quite so satisfying as getting into a groove and connecting on a fusillade of jumpers. A shot of moderate backspin and arc that swishes through will be briefly checked, dropped to the ground with a residue of rotation, and returned in a series of bounces of diminishing height. It's as if the reward for accuracy is the net's playing valet. But when playing at netless rims, a swish is never followed by a bowling-alley ball return. The shot follows an unimpeded path, and the myopic easily mistake it for an airball. Even though the ball's backspin will slow its progress once it lands, chances are the shooter will have to trace his shot's route overland before he can again cradle the ball in his hands.

The rhythm of a groove seems capricious in the way it comes and—as soon as company arrives or a game begins—goes. But the basketball player, like the guy in the batting cage who gets sick of Iron Mike after a while, and the tennis player, who can take a bangboard for only so long, knows that he'll eventually have to test himself against someone else.

One-on-One

Your playground survival training course begins with One-on-One. Even the most team-oriented player can benefit from a few One-on-One classes in order to add some potential face jobs to his repertoire. Whatever pet move you have in mind and want to perfect—a running hook, a double pump, a scoop shot, or any one of the many variations of the game's more standard shots—this is your chance to master it under game conditions. Remember: The most important trait of the good One-on-One player is the ability to get a shot off at will.

One-on-One prepares you for the playground in a way that goes beyond skill. It builds character. It's you against him, your every weakness is exposed, and if you lose there's only one scapegoat. Sure, unless you're a Van Arsdale and your regular foe is your twin brother, most One-on-One matches are inherently unfair. The key is to minimize your disadvantages and work what edge you've got

Blocking out is important in One-on-One, since if you do box your opponent from the boards, you're essentially guaranteed a bound.

to the hilt. The mismatches in height and speed that come up, the discrepancies in physical strength—they're all part of One-on-One.

On defense, position is most important. If you must try for a steal, the safest move is to jab with one hand when your man is facing you. If you lunge, beware—you may end up watching an uncontested lay-up. Blocking out is deceptively important in One-on-One, since if you *do* box your opponent from the boards, you're essentially guaranteed a bound.

When you've got the ball, form your game plan intelligently. If you're the smaller player and own a quick, accurate outside shot, stay out around the key area; dribble along the periphery and pull the trigger on bombs. If you happen to be off target, long rebounds—which you'll have a better chance to snatch than the short ones—may come your way. Work on shots you're sure to get off, even over much taller adversaries; hooks and fallaways, for instance, are more likely to work than straight jumpers. And, the same way a good pitcher sets up his fast ball with a curve, you can set up a drive to the hoop with several outside shots. If you're strong and quick, and especially if the rim or backboard is loose or low, try making an explosive three-step, one-dribble move after the ball is checked. And if you've got the edge in height, or if you release the ball from safely behind your head, try backing into the lane and throwing up delicate turnaround jumpers.

Or, rather than following precise stratagems for One-on-One play, simply let your imagination take you where it might. Don't be overly concerned with the final score, unless you're playing out a grudge match; this is your opportunity to play without being bothered with passing or screening or the whining of teammates who want the ball. Work on developing your game with an eye toward that moment when you'll pull a facial in a full-court affair.

Two-on-Two

At first glance, Two-on-Two might seem like little more than two players taking turns at One-on-One. Don't catch yourself with that attitude; you'll end up standing around and watching instead of playing. Instead, begin putting the elements of team play together. Learn how to use the pick-and-roll. If you should set a pick, roll, and not get the ball even though you're free, let your teammate know about it.

Defensively, look for chances to double-team when your opponents come together. Here, unlike in a One-on-One match, you

OPPOSITE PAGE:
If you're strong and quick, try making an explosive three-step, one-dribble move after the ball is checked.

Don't catch yourself with this attitude—that Two-on-Two is little more than two players taking turns at One-on-One.

don't have to make a clean steal to come up with the ball; if you merely tip it loose, your partner may come away with it. Offensive rebounding skills can also be developed in Two-on-Two. While your partner is wheeling and dealing, look to get rebounding position on the weak side of the court, away from the ball. Also begin working on the back-door play. If all this seems too orthodox, like something out of a coaching text, remember that the alley-oop is the playground, hang glider's back-door—and all it takes is two.

Three-on-Three

Three-on-Three is the classic half-court match-up, featuring a beautiful balance between the individual and the collective. Even in full-court "runs," only three of the five offensive players are usually involved at any one time; as a result, Three-on-Three simulates many Five-on-Five patterns.

In Three-on-Three, you begin to use the entire court. You can set picks on the ball or away from it. You can run crisscross patterns. And you can set up a three-man, give-from-one-side-go-from-the-other back-door. Three-on-Three also sees the development of guard and forward play. Big guys must learn to establish position down low, receive a pass, and operate with the ball inside. Playground guards reach puberty not by popping twenty-foot jumpers, but by penetrating the lane with their quickness. But it's position and savvy, not quickness and strength, that mark the best Three-on-Three players. Suddenly there's a weak side, so get in the habit of using that dimension of the court, of passing and screening away from your pass.

Three-on-Three: The classic half-court match-up.

Four-on-Four

This 400-level class is a graduate course in half-court ball. With eight players confined to only half the court, and with the action concentrated within the key area, congestion forces the playground student to develop some court sense and awareness. On defense you just begin to get physical, especially inside. *Selectively* leave your feet; you'll begin to refine the art of rejection, and, should you get burned with a head fake, there are now three teammates who can help out. Four-on-Four also provides a great opportunity to get some offensive movement into your game. A good jump shooter can be murder in some knock-around shooting game, but will be ineffective in half-court unless he can get free for his shots on his own.

Since there are now thirty-two limbs out there, Four-on-Four provides a chance to learn how to cope with contact. If you're an inside player, work on muscling: Giving a head fake, going up strongly, *and* putting it in. (Remember, there'll be no zebra with a whistle nearby to send you to the line.) Forwards who enjoy driving can perfect the art of getting a shot off in traffic. And penetrating guards should polish their passing skills. Occasionally you'll find Four-on-Four played full-court. But most such matches degenerate into sloppy affairs unless the court is short. Your best bet is to wait for two more players to come before running full.

Position and savvy make the best Three-on-Three players.

Five-on-Five

While Three-on-Three is the classic half-court playground game, full-court Five-on-Five is the ultimate test. Every other game played and all the hours spent playing alone lead into the "run." The weaker points of your game will quickly show themselves when you run full-court. Suddenly they're no longer just your liabilities but your teammates' as well. Keep the score in mind; pride is often on the line in a full-court face-off. More than anything else, Five-on-Five is a winner's game.

Accordingly, if you're out of shape, politely decline the proffered invitation, "Wanna run?" If it once was the sharp-edged voice of a coach which exhorted you to grab that rebound or go to the basket, now peer pressure does the same with calls to "rise" or "do it." Players at the top of the playground hierarchy often limit their court appearances to Five-on-Five, which is another indication of the high plateau on which this game sits. The congratulatory expression "good run" is reserved solely for the winners of a Five-on-Five contest.

Four-on-Four means congestion in the lane, even during a grade school recess game.

H-O-R-S-E

No one knows who the Edison was who invented H-O-R-S-E, but whoever he was, he saw the creative potential of basketball and likely believed in the doctrine of "If you spell it, you are one."

The rules of the game don't vary much from region to region. Just as in billiards, player "A" announces his shot precisely as he intends to enact it. If he's called "straight in" before shooting and the shot goes in off the backboard, it doesn't count. If player "A" *does* make his shot, as he spelled it out, player "B" is charged with exactly duplicating the maneuver. Should "B" also complete the shot successfully, no penalty letter is charged to either player and "A," having retained the lead, shoots again from a spot of his choice. But if "B" misses the prescribed shot, he picks up a penalty letter. "B" can gain the "lead"—that is, the chance to force penalty letters on "A"—only after an unsuccessful shot by "A." When one player has received enough penalty letters to spell out the word *horse*, the game is over and the unsaddled player declared the winner.

Virtually any number can play; the rules remain the same, and play rotates until the process of elimination yields a winner. Obviously, it's to your advantage to follow a weak player in the order—it allows you to gain the lead more often. You'll soon discover that two types of players tend to dominate games of H-O-R-S-E. The first is the outside shooter with good range. The second is the player who has developed a series of trick shots, some especially for H-O-R-S to H-O-R-S deadlocks. Trick shots come in all varieties and regularly include the use of props and working the ball around the back, through the legs, and off the head. Players with an exceptionally soft touch will chime "swish" when announcing their shot. (That means that the shot need only be matched if it's a swish—but if it *does* hit nothing but bottom, it must be duplicated without rim or backboard.) Those who have mastered the geometry of backboard angles will chant "off the board" before certain shots. And still others will routinely sink shots from out-of-bounds, from a curb or stair, or even from behind the backboard. And while in the televised H-O-R-S-E competition the late Mendy Rudolph shielded many NBA stars from embarrassment with his ban on repeating the same trick shot in any one game, no similar restriction shelters playground H-O-R-S-E players. There is, however, an unwritten rule against dunking, unless everyone participating can jam.

Many prefer to play O-U-T, an abridged version of H-O-R-S-E. The rules remain the same. In fact, feel free to choose whatever

word you like. If you have plenty of time on your hands, maybe A-N-T-I-D-I-S-E-S-T-A-B-L-I-S-H-M-E-N-T-A-R-I-A-N-I-S-M   is for you (though keeping track of the score will be hard); on the other hand, if you number yourself among the members of the If You Spell It, You Are One School, challenge a nemesis to a game of S-U-C-K-E-R. And you may want to put a little charity into your game: Before your opponent accepts his final letter, after missing your behind-the-back, full-360-degree twist, off-the-backboard tap shot, grant him another chance.

Full-court Five-on-Five: The ultimate test.

Around the World

If you can't seem to beat the trick-shot artists at H-O-R-S-E but have a pretty decent outside shot, Around the World is for you. It's the classic shooter's game. Great for when you're tired after half- or full-court play, it too can accommodate several players.

The most common rules specify that the first player start with a shot from the right baseline. If you miss the first try, it's the next player's turn. If you sink it, you advance to the next spot, about five feet to the left, where you have a banking angle. Toss that one

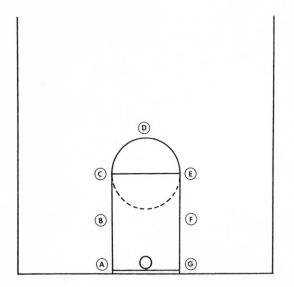

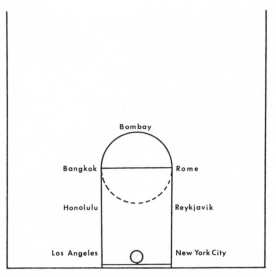

in—from the spot marked B on the diagram—and you move again, this time a step back from where the foul lane and line meet. Your circumnavigation continues across the top of the key and along the far side of the lane, and then back again along the other "hemisphere." The first player returning to spot A is the winner, but each player is permitted the same number of turns—which often keeps the possibility of an overtime alive.

Most include a "do or die" element in Around the World, allowing players to "risk it" or "chance it" after they miss their first try from a particular spot. If you risk it and score, you advance to the next space; if you miss, you return to square one (and do not pass GO and do not collect $200). Or you may simply "pass," in which case possession reverts to your opponent and you stay where you are. There are many variations of the game; some play with a left-handed lay-up leading off and a right-handed one preceding the return trip. Still others play that, if you risk it and miss, you need only go back one space, or that you can risk it a third time with the entire game on the line. These riders can be added at the participants' discretion.

A soft-drink manufacturer recently commercialized Around the World as a promotional gimmick, but if you're a purist with a geographical or political bent you can make more worthwhile adjustments. Try taking the game literally, and assign a name to each spot on the court. All the cities in the diagram, for instance, are roughly equidistant from one another. In L.A., try a finger roll in honor of Wilt Chamberlain. Add a little wiggle to your form in

Honolulu. Bangkok calls for something exotic—a wild hook or underhanded number, for example. Let go an ascetic set shot from Bombay; you might incant sections of the Bhagavad-Gita to heighten your concentration. When in Rome, do what Nero let the city do—burn. If you want to try something unpredictable—or simply quit—do it in Reykjavík, as Bobby Fischer would. And a straight double-pump would do New York City proud.

Twenty-one

After H-O-R-S-E and Around the World, Twenty-one is probably the most popular of the so-called knock-around games. The rules vary, depending on where you're from, and, naturally enough, the first player to reach twenty-one points is the winner.

Play begins with a foul shot, and the shooter receives two points if he sinks it. Regardless of whether the foul shot is successful or not, the player retrieves his own rebound on one bounce and, *from the exact spot where it is collected,* takes a second shot. If this falls, he gets one point. As long as a player makes both shots he continues to shoot, always returning to the foul line after a successful

follow-up. When the chain is broken, with a player missing either or both of his two tries, the next player takes his turn.

Most games of Twenty-one are governed by several additional rules. Many play that each contestant must "break the ice," or sink at least one foul shot, before he can begin scoring or avail himself of follow-up shots. Most games also require that a player work his score so it lands precisely on twenty-one. (This may involve perfecting that un-American technique of intentionally missing a shot.) Others play that a player missing both his foul and rebound shots—after breaking the ice—will have his score revert to zero and the "icebreaker" clause reimposed. Twenty-one can also be played by more than two, and, like Around the World, each player is permitted the same number of turns. This always ensures the possibility of a comeback, even with the score twenty-zip. Keep in mind that, since the shot that breaks the ice can't score any points, all it takes are seven perfect series to hit twenty-one exactly.

Five-Three-One

Five-Three-One is a variation on the Twenty-one theme. After breaking the ice from the top of the key, the first player shoots again from that spot, with five points at stake. Whether his shot falls or not, he retrieves the rebound on one bounce, shoots again for three points, and grabs the next rebound. He then takes his last shot, worth one point. If he's made all three shots—in other words, scored nine points—he returns to the top of the key and keeps shooting. Otherwise, it's the next player's turn to break the ice and start scoring. Remember: The five-pointer is always taken from the top of the circle, and the three- and one-point shots from wherever the rebounds end up. If you miss all three shots in a turn, your slate reads zilch. Again, most play that you have to hit twenty-one exactly.

Sets and Taps

There's no question that Sets and Taps owes its origin to the city playgrounds. If you've ever marveled at those players who grab rebounds and, before returning to the pavement, release shots, here's how to play the game that may have been their training tool:

Player "A" starts things off, usually from around the top of the key, by taking a jump shot. (Yes, the game's called Sets and Taps, not Jumps and Taps, but styles change faster than names.) One point is awarded for each basket from out here, once the ice has been broken. Player "B" positions himself somewhere in the lane, preparing himself to grab and shoot, or tap, one of "A's" missed shots. (However the tapper does it, he must gain control of the ball after leaving his feet and let a shot go before returning to earth.) If player "B" succeeds, two points become his, as does the opportunity to shoot jumpers. Should the shooter miss three in a row, he forfeits his turn. The game is played to a predetermined score, usually that all-purpose number, twenty-one. Though the game can be played by just two players, three is ideal, since it supplies a tapper for each side of the lane. The rebounding struggles help everyone's game. Advice for shooters: Low, line-drive shots are the toughest to tip.

Seven-Up

Two or more players form a semicircle at an agreed-upon distance from the hoop, and everyone shoots in turn. The number of letters you receive *when* you miss will equal the number of shots that have gone in *before* you miss. Seven letters spell S-E-V-E-N-U-P and you're out. When good shooters are playing, the game can be especially dramatic, with pressure building after every basket.

Knock-out

If you're all alone, waiting for someone to come by against whom you can go one-on-one, but—alas! doesn't it always happen this way?—*two* players come along, don't despair. There's always Knock-out. Two players take the court and go one-on-one until someone scores. The winner remains on the court—and keeps possession of the ball—as the challenger rises for his turn. Everyone keeps his own score. The player sitting out can normally do little more than verbally harass those playing. But, on the playground, that's a worthwhile skill to develop.

Scuttlebutt

This is another game for more than two players, sometimes called Free-for-All, Animal Ball, or Roughhouse. Play proceeds like One-on-One or Knock-out, but here the player with the ball must contend with more defenders. Each player keeps his own score. With every change of possession, play simply continues, with the new offensive player challenging the two or more defenders. A field goal scored from outside a fifteen-foot radius from the hoop is worth two points; a basket sunk from within that area counts one. Games go to—you guessed it—twenty-one, but when one player reaches eleven, anyone with less than three points is forced into early retirement. You must hit twenty-one on the nose to win. Should a player exceed that barrier, his score reverts to thirteen and play continues.

Fight Thirty-one

This is another version of Scuttlebutt, sometimes called Varsity. It's essentially Scuttlebutt, only there are no boundaries on loose balls and score is kept to thirty-one. (If a player with the ball should go out of bounds, the defenders shoot fingers among themselves to see who'll get possession.) Play in both these games often becomes quite intense, with plenty of arguing. If you don't have the ball, let the third and fourth players play tight defense. That way you'll get a step's advantage toward the basket and a rebound.

Fight 31, like Scuttlebutt, means One-on-One-on-One.

Fouls

When you've just finished a day of serious ballplaying, and you feel as though camera crews will be by imminently to shoot a Miller commercial, relax a bit with a game of Fouls. The rules are elementary: Each player shoots twenty foul shots and the player sinking the most wins. But wins what? Fouls is never played just for the fun of it; something must be at stake . . . a beer, a soda, or just an ice cream cone. Heckling, funny faces, and elaborate ways of breaking the shooter's rhythm when returning the ball are all part of the game.

3. ASPHALT ARGOT

"A fifth" is found on the sidelines, not in a liquor store

THE vernacular of the organized game has combined with street slang to give playground basketball a language of its own. The pick-up game breeds colorful phrases and nicknames, truncating words like "competition" and "reputation" into "comp" and "rep," and "elbow" and "goaltending" into "bow" and "tending." It turns a pronoun as simple as "you" into an urgent call to make a move or hit a jumper. And where else but on a playground would you hear something as clannish as "Take who takes you" or "Do you need a fifth?"

In the heat of a game, there isn't time for much more than the one- and two-word shouts that serve to alert and orient teammates. "Switch!" "Get back!" "Ball!" "Turn!" "Help!" "Stay!" and "Ball's in!" are all defensive signals. "Trailer!" "Roll!" and "Foul line!" are just as economically meaningful, but you hear them on offense. Rebounders react to "Shot!" "Same team!" and "Short!"—the last an exclamation from a shooter warning teammates that his shot will hit either the front rim or nothing at all. (Since "Short!" always provides new information to one more opponent than teammate, its primary function is to save *some* face—by showing the world that you *know* when you've uncorked an air-ball.)

Language is often the key to gaining a psychological edge on an opponent. Floyd Brady, a legendary New England playground figure, instinctively yells "All night!" when a teammate shoots, and "Not today!" when an opponent lets fly. Larry Hollyfield, a legend in his own right in Southern California, taunts "Too late!" as he lets his jumper go and a tardy defender comes over to block it. Many New York City street players yell their school's name—or number—as they drive the lane: "Watch out for [P.S.] 118!" And it's only logical that, after someone unleashes a *brick*, an opponent adds, "Bring out the mortar!"

Here's a sampling of that unique dialect:

Ad (*n*) Advantage. When one team has a basket's edge and the next score will win a game, the squad a shot away from victory is said to have the advantage, or *ad.* If the trailing team gets that next score, the *count* reverts to *deuce.* Cf. *deuce, game point, up.*

Airball (*n*) A shot that touches neither rim nor backboard, this is the ultimate humiliation. It's like getting sand kicked in your face at the beach in front of your girl friend, only there aren't any comic-book coupon remedies. Only practice helps. Syn. *house*; cf. *swish.*

All net (*n*) See *swish.*

Apple (*n*) See *pill.*

Ball (*n*) 1. The thing the game is played with. 2. Basketball, the game. Real aficionados find the prefix "basket" superfluous. Syn. *hoop.*

Basketball Jones (*n*) An affliction of the bone marrow. Under certain conditions, the marrow begins stirring and the patient must play ball. A song of the same name celebrated the addiction.

Blitz (*v*) See *skunk.*

Bogart (*v*) To make a strong move on someone inside.

Boogie (*v*) To drive.

Bound (*n* or *v*) Rebound. Syn. *Pull, snatch, yank.*

Bow (*n*) Elbow. Bows are thrown to settle scores and get position.

Box (*n*) 1. A tape player or radio. Boxes, which play tunes, are standard in many city parks. And the music they play invokes muses that inspire many a memorable move. 2. The foul lane area. Syn. *death valley, office.*

LEFT:
Throwing a bow *to get position.*

RIGHT:
Making a check, *up top.*

The box: *Court-side companion and sixth man.*

Break the ice (*v*) This rite of making at least one shot before you can begin scoring is common to most schoolyard shooting games.
Brick (*n*) A shot with little backspin, accuracy, or chance of going in. **Bricklayer.**
Bring it up (*v*) See *take it out.*

Buckets (*n*) This is the type of half-court game in which a shot can be rebounded and put right back up without the need to *take it around*. A modified version only allows *airballs* to go right back up. Syn. *city ball, Lincoln, New York, straight up.*

Bunny (*n*) See *chippie.*

Burn (*v*) 1. To score, usually on several shots in succession. 2. To beat, especially beat badly, with a single move. 3. To win convincingly. Syn. *use;* cf. *get burned.*

Bush (*adj*) Cheap or without class; dirty. A *submarine* is considered bush.

Bus stop (*n*) A jump shot.

Bust (*n*) A strong move to the hoop.

Butcher (*n or v*) 1. A defender who uses force rather than finesse. 2. To inflict physical punishment on another player. Syn. *hack, hacker.*

Camp (*v*) To establish steadfast position under the basket.

Can (*v*) See *drill.*

Change of hands (*n*) The rules governing a half-court game in which the ball must be brought back beyond a certain point, usually the foul line, once it has changed hands after a rebound or turnover. Syn. *Washington;* cf. *buckets, take it around.*

Check (*n or v*) 1. In half-court ball, the custom of letting a defender *out front* handle the ball briefly before it is inbounded to be sure the defensive team is ready. 2. A blocked shot. A shot hitting the bottom of the rim is sometimes called a *self check.* Syn. *gate, grill, rejection, snuff, stuff.*

Cherry picking (*n*) In a full-court game, the technique of laying back on defense, or basket-hanging, to get a head start on a fast break. Syn. *snowbirding.*

Chinese basket (*n*) A shot that enters the basket from the bottom of the cylinder before dropping back through. According to "the rules," it doesn't count.

Chippie (*n*) The name for a very short, simple shot is derived from golf's term for the same. Syn. *bunny.*

Chucker (*n*) A player who shoots a lot, especially from distant and awkward positions. Cf. *gunner, heaver, pump.*

Chump (*n*) A weak player, especially a weak opponent. The difference between champ and chump, one playground taunt goes, is *u.*

City ball (*n*) See *buckets.*

Clearance (*n*) In a half-court game played according to *change of hands,* the ball must be taken beyond a certain spot with every new possession. *Side clearance* is roughly fifteen to twenty feet from the basket in the corners; *back clearance* is to the foul line or beyond. Cf. *take it around, change of hands.*

Comp (*n*) Competition.

Count (*n*) The score. Like those housewives who watch "Dialing for Dollars," if you're playing for money, keep in mind the count and the amount.

Counterfeit (*adj*) A shot that's neither likely—nor deserves—to go in is described this way.

Courtesy (*n*) If you sink a shot while warming up, according to this chivalric code, you get another. Rebounders owe you return passes until you miss. Courtesy is usually not extended for lay-ups or very short jumpers—though often for *airballs,* to give the goat a chance to redeem himself. Syn. *follows*; cf. *rules of the court.*

Cup (*n*) The rim. Syn. *rack, hole.*

Cutting each other up (*v*) When two schoolyard stars get locked in a duel, this is what they do to one another, trying to outdo one facial with the next.

D (*n*) Defense.

Day (*n*) Whiteness. Cf. *night.*

Deal (*v*) To pass fancily, usually off a fast break. Wheeling and dealing means a spin move or tricky dribble has been thrown in. Cf. *operate.*

Death Valley (*n*) The foul lane area, where hackers lie in waiting. Syn. *box, office.*

Delay Dunk (*n*) See *rub-in.*

Deuce (*adj*) Playground *hoop* learned this from its more patrician cousin, tennis: The score is tied and "you gotta win by two." Cf. *ad, game point, up.*

Dipsy-do (*n*) A short double-pumped shot, usually let go underhanded.

Dish (*n* or *v*) 1. To pass off neatly; to make an assist. 2. A pass that leads to a basket.

Doctor (*n*) A player who *operates* and makes *house calls.*

Do it (*v*) Making a graceful offensive maneuver, usually off a fast break or from outside, and with finesse rather than power. Cf. *freak out, get back, operate, take it to him.*

Do or die (*v*) There's not quite so much as life and death at stake when this shot, to decide which team will get possession, goes up. Sometimes whatever is on the line is decided *from* the line (but, more often, from the top of the key). Syn. *hit or miss, make it take it.*

Down (*adj*) 1. If you're down for the next game, you have *winners* or *nexts.* 2. To be behind in the *count.* Cf. *up.*

Down low (*prep* or *adv*) See *underneath.*

Downtown (*prep* or *adv*) Way outside; roughly, the three-point field goal region.

Dunk (*n* or *v*) Oh come on. You know what this is. Syn. *jam, slam, stuff, take, throwdown;* cf. *funk dunk, punk dunk.*

D up (*v*) A call to play, or tighten up on, defense.

Eat it (*v*) See *taste that.*

Face (*n*) That intangible at stake in first-rate playground encounters that makes even single plays memorable. When face is at stake, you can do only one of two things: save it or lose it. Syn. *service.*

Face job (*n*) A individual offensive or defensive move so captivating that it wins, for one player for one moment, the kharma of *face.* Syn. *facial, Noxzema.*

Facial (*n*) See *face job.*

Fall back (*v*) See *scoot.*

Feel (*n*) A *check,* usually *out front.*

Fill it up (*v*) To score on a succession of shots, usually from the outside.

Firsts (*n*) Without a referee, when two players tie each other up in what would otherwise be a jump ball, the player to yell "firsts" first gains possession. Cf. *shoot for it.*

Flush (*v*) To score. Cf. *toilet seater.*

Follows (*n*) See *courtesy.*

Freak out (*v*) When Fly McDuitt is loose on a fast break, with only Sammy Suburban back on defense, this would be the cry to Fly from throughout the park. Cf. *do it, get back, operate, pay back, take it to him.*

Free ins (*n*) In cramped suburban driveways, games are often played according to free-ins: Defenders may not intercept the first inbounds pass, nor may they harass the inbounder.

Funk dunk (*n*) Any sort of *dunk* that showcases flair or leaping ability.

Game (*n*) 1. The sport. 2. A single contest. 3. With a possessive pronoun, indicates who has the privilege to play next ("It's my game") or a player's style ("His game is all left-hand"). Cf. *down, up, winners.*

The Garbageman's Law *holds that just about anything can be trashed.*

Game point (*n*) When a game has reached the juncture where the team with the ball can win the game with one score, the potential basket is said to represent game point. Cf. *ad, deuce, up.*

Garbage (*n*) A loose ball or rebound that results in a lay-up or short jumper. Cf. *garbageman's law, junk.*

Garbageman's Law (*n*) Backboard plus Spin equals Basket. Apply it, and you'll find just about anything can be trashed. Cf. *garbage, junk.*

Gate (*n* or *v*) 1. To stymie; figuratively to shut the gate on someone. 2. A blocked shot. Syn. *check, grill, rejection, snuff, stuff.*

Get back (*v*) 1. To retreat on defense. 2. If you've been *burned* by an opponent, your teammates will yell this and get you the ball, in the hope that you can redeem yourself. Syn. *payback;* cf. *do it, freak out, operate, take it to him.*

Get burned (*v*) 'Tis better to *burn* than get burned. Cf. *burn.*

Grease it (*v*) A cry heard from shooters whose shots are hanging on the rim.

Grill (*n* or *v*) See *gate*.

Gunner (*n*) A player who enjoys shooting. Connotes some degree of success. Cf. *chucker, heaver, pump*.

Gusjohnson (*v*) To *dunk* so ferociously that rim is separated from backboard. (Ex-pro Gus Johnson did it once.) I *gusjohnson*, you *gusjohnson*, he *gusjohnsons*, we *gusjohnson*. "The basket be broke, 'cause he done *gusjohnsoned* it."

Hacker (*n*) See *butcher*.

Handle (*n*) A player with deft ball-handling skills is said to have a good handle.

Heaver (*n*) A player with little shooting skill. Cf. *chucker, gunner, pump*.

A player with deft ball-handling skills is said to have a good handle.

Hit (*n* or *v*) 1. A successful shot, which has usually followed a path of low trajectory, or been banked in. 2. To score.

Hit or miss (*v*) See *do or die*.

Hold court (*v*) To remain in successive *pick-up games* by virtue of consecutive victories. Cf. *winners*.

Hole (*n*) See *cup*.

Hoop (*n*) 1. A scored basket. 2. The basket apparatus itself. 3. The sport of basketball; also, *hoops*. Syn. *ball*.

House (*n*) See *airball*.

House call (*n*) A showy and successful move; something a *doctor* would do.

In your eye (*prep*) See *in your face*.

In your face (*prep*) The taunt uttered after the execution of a *face job*. You're entitled to say this after scoring a shot despite tight defense, or after returning a shot in an opponent's face. Syn. *in your eye, in your mug*.

In your mug (*prep*) See *in your face*.

Jam (*n* or *v*) See *dunk*.

Juke (*n* or *v*) A sudden move used by either an offensive or a defensive player, usually as a decoy. May be part of *wheeling and dealing* or a defensive ploy.

Junk (*n*) An awkward or unusual shot not normally in the shooter's repertoire; may be outmoded set shots, spin shots, or even *garbage*. Cf. *garbage*.

Lincoln (*n*) See *buckets*.

L'l Help (*n*) The playground S.O.S. If your ball rolls away toward a neighboring game or gets stuck in a tangled chain net, this alerts others that you'd like them to retrieve it or offer their ball to jar yours free. (Whatever you do, though, don't utter the annoyingly presumptuous "Thank you!" that's heard around country clubs.)

Load up (*v*) The techinque of manipulating the *pick-up* process to give your team a distinct edge, or calling *winners* and inviting only the strongest players to join you. Syn. *stack;* cf. *pick-up, winners*.

Look (*n* or *v*) 1. A pass, usually to a player inside, that leads to a basket. 2. To pass inside. Cf. *dish*.

Losers (*n*) 1. In half-court ball, this is the system where possession goes to the team that surrenders a basket. 2. The people you try not to be when *face* is at stake. Cf. *winners*.

Make it take it (*v*) See *winners, do or die.*

Man (*n*) 1. An opponent who is being defended. 2. An abbreviation for man-to-man defense. 3. A protégé or fellow player. "My man" indicates, roughly, "my partner"; "my main man" indicates "my principal partner."

Match (*n or v*) The rules of match often govern the process of shooting to decide who'll get first possession, and who will play if there is an uneven number, or surplus, of prospective players. If the first shooter hits, his counterpart must match the shot; otherwise, possession or the right to play belongs to the first shooter. The basis for the game H-O-R-S-E, which is a succession of matches. Cf. *shoot for it.*

Meminger's Law (*n*) An edict promulgated by New York schoolyard product and former pro Dean Meminger. It decrees that, if you don't play ball, you can't hang out.

New York (*n*) See *buckets.*

Nexts (*n*) See *winners.*

Night (*n*) Blackness or funk. Cf. *day.*

Nothing but bottom (*n*) See *all net.*

Noxzema (*n*) See *face job.*

Office (*n*) The lane area. Syn. *box, death valley.*

Operate (*v*) *Doing it* in close quarters. Where *do it* usually applies to action off a fast break or from *out front,* operation is work near the hoop. Technique is not taught at med schools. Cf. *do it, doctor, freak out, house call, take it to him.*

Out front (*prep or adv*) The area beyond the foul line where the ball is *checked* after each basket, foul, or turnover. This region is a half court's backcourt. Syn. *up top.*

Outs (*n*) Possession. After hitting a shot in a half-court contest played according to the *winners* system, the scorer can rightfully claim, "It's my outs."

Palm (*n or v*) 1. To hold the ball in one hand, usually for show. Obligatory for most varieties of *funk dunk.* 2. The illegal dribble on which there's no prohibition in the speakeasies of the schoolyards.

Pay back (*v*) See *get back.*

Pearl (*n*) A move you wouldn't be ashamed to take uptown, well past Ninety-fifth Street. Believers in the Earl Monroe Doctrine may throw in a spin and some *wheeling and dealing.*

Pick-up (*adj* or *v*) Unorganized or without prior planning. *Pick-up ball* is played by players who have gathered without the fore-knowledge of how teams would appear. The term comes from the process of choosing or picking up teams from those present. *Pick-up Game, Pick-up Team.*

Pill (*n*) The ball. Parents needn't worry if Junior is *popping* pills in the schoolyard. Syn. *apple, rock.*

Play house (*v*) To establish dominance *underneath* or—to mix a metaphor—in the *office.*

Point game (*n*) See *game point.*

Pop (*n* or *v*) 1. To shoot a jumper suddenly. 2. A quickly released jump shot.

Possession (*n*) See *winners.*

Prayer (*n*) A shot let go in such desperation that it seems that only divine intervention can put it in the basket.

Pull (*n* or *v*) See *bound.*

Sometimes it takes a shout of "Push it up" to get a fast break into high gear.

Pump (*n*) A player who shoots often with little success and selfishly does so. Cf. *Chucker, gunner, heaver.*

Punk dunk (*n*) Any sort of *dunk* that humiliates the defender.

Push it up (*v*) Yell this when you want the ball to be brought quickly into the forecourt.

Rack (*n*) See *cup.*

Rattle (*n*) A successful shot where the ball hits the inside of the rim two or three times before dropping through. Cf. *drill, hit, pop, swish.*

Rejection (*n*) A convincingly blocked shot that comes back via the same path it's put up. Syn. *check, gate, grill, snuff, stuff.*

Rep (*n*) Reputation.

Rip (*n*) A successful shot, usually a *swish.* Cf. *drill, hit, pop, rattle, swish.*

Rise (*v*) See *sky.*

Rock (*n* or *v*) 1. The ball. Syn. *pill.* 2. To play ball. Cf. *boogie.*

Rub-in (*n*) A wishy-washy dunk that fudges around the rim. Avoid. Syn. *delay dunk.*

Rules of the court (*n*) A convention of warming up in which players shoot until they miss and then take a lay-up. Cf. *courtesy.*

Run (*n*) A full-court game, not a twenty-six-mile, three-hundred-and-whatever-yard course. When you're asked, "Wanna run?" you're being asked to play ball, not go jogging. And "good run" would denote "nice game," not a best seller.

Run a clinic (*v*) 1. To execute a crisp play, with two or more players, that results in a basket. 2. To win convincingly, by scoring predominantly via back doors, alley-oops, and give-and-gos.

Run and gun (*n*) The quintessential fast-break, inner-city offense.

Run it back (*v*) The request of a *pick-up team* that, though just beaten, wants an immediate re-match. If another squad has *winners*, the request won't be granted (unless the players on deck are consensus chumps, in which case "run it back" may mean "let's pretend we never finished, and keep playing").

Scoop (*n* or *v*) To swish a shot from outside. The basket is a bin of ice cream; the shooter is simply serving himself a cone. The Double Dip Dunk comes from this metaphor, very much extended. Cf. *swish.*

Scoot (*v*) A player's call to his teammates to retreat on defense, because he knows his shot's going to drop. Syn. *fall back.*

Self check (*n* or *v*) See *check.*

Send it (*v*) The *cherry picker*'s call to a rebounder to let go an outlet pass.

Service (*n*) See *face.*

Sewer (*n*) A basket so accommodating that everything going near it goes down it.

Shake (*v*) To elude an opponent, usually by tempting.him with a stutterstep or *juke* and then bursting away. *Shake and bake* means to tantalize, elude, and *burn.* Cf. *burn, juke.*

Shake and bake (*v*) See *shake.*

Shirts (*n*) See *shirts 'n' skins.*

Shirts 'n' skins (*n*) A means of distinguishing one team from another without using uniforms. Members of one team keep their shirts on while the others remove theirs. Has yet to reach wide acceptance among women.

Shoot for it (*v*) 1. When faced with a jump ball or other quandry and no referee is available, two players—one from each team—shoot fingers or take shots to determine who'll get possession. 2. A way of forming teams. The first two, three, four, or five to hit usually form one team; the next group to hit makes up the opposition. Cf. *match.*

Skins (*n*) See *shirts 'n' skins.*

Skunk (*v*) To beat an opponent by shutting him out is known as skunking. Many half-court games set to go to eleven or fifteen will end at seven if only one party has scored. If your foe begins sniffing conspicuously in the midst of a game, check on the score; if it's six to *zip,* he probably thinks some schoolyard euthanasia is imminent. Syn. *blitz.*

Sky (*v*) Not merely to jump, but to sail—in pursuit of *hoops, bounds, rejections,* or rarer air. Syn. *rise, talk to God.*

Skywalk (*n* or *v*) 1. To perform a leaping move with shoulders somewhere around rim level. 2. The aerial stroll itself.

Slam (*n* or *v*) See *dunk.*

Snatch (*n* or *v*) See *bound.*

Snowbirding (*v*) See *cherry picking.*

Snuff (*n* or *v*) See *gate.*

Stack (*v*) See *load up.*

Stick (*v*) See *drill.*

Straight (*adj*) You don't have to win by two when you play a game *straight.* Cf. *deuce.*

Straight up (*n*) See *buckets.*

Stretch it out (*v*) Roughly translated, means "go full court."

A snuff is a stuff, with just a little extra.

Stuff (*n* or *v*) 1. *Dunk.* Syn. *jam, slam, take, throwdown.* 2. Block. Syn. *check, gate, grill, rejection, snuff.*

Submarine (*n* or *v*) To get in front of a player's feet after he has left them on a drive to the basket. It's a dangerous move, whose aim is often to maim. Sometimes starts fights.

Swish (*n*) A shot that twinkles only twine, avoiding backboard and rim. Syn. *all net, nothing but bottom;* cf. *scoop.*

Take (*n* or *v*) 1. *Dunk.* Syn. *jam, slam, stuff, throwdown.* 2. To guard, as in "take who takes you."

Take it around (*v*) The bringing of the ball into the backcourt in a half-court game played according to *change of hands.* Syn. *take it back*; cf. *clearance, change of hands.*

Shooting The J.

Take it back (*v*) See *take it around.*

Take it out (*v*) To inbound the ball. Syn. *bring it up.*

Take it to him (*v*) A suburban rendering of the urban *do it* or *freak out.* Cf. *do it, freak out, get back, operate, pay back.*

Takers (*n*) See *make it take it.*

Take the train (*v*) A less-than-diplomatic suggestion that someone has traveled. Variations include "Take the A train," "Take the El," "Take the Amtrak," and "Take the Greyhound," depending on which part of the country you call home. (A more diplomatic way to call steps: "I believe I heard the pitter-patter of little feet.")

Talk to God (*v*) See *sky.*

Taste that (*v*) After blocking an opponent's shot, say this to remind him what he can do with it. Syn. *eat it.*

Tending (*v*) Goaltending. When in the *office*, one often tends to affairs.

The J (*n*) The jump shot. *J Up, Shoot the J.*

Three-sixty (*n*) A shot off a drive in which the shooter spins 360 degrees in the air between takeoff and landing, and releases the ball before returning to earth. Syn. *whirlybird.*

Throwdown (*n*) See *dunk. Throw It Down.*

Toilet seater (*n*) A shot that rolls around the rim several times before dropping through or rolling out. Cf. *flush.*

Tree (*n*) A tall player.

Twine (*n*) Net. The root for the expressions "twine time" and "twine twinkler."

Underneath (*prep* or *adv*) The area along the baseline and under the basket, where *doctors operate.* Syn. *down low;* cf. *death valley.*

Up (*adj*) 1. "All"; with a number, indicates that the score is tied. Cf. *ad, deuce, game point.* 2. A person or team that has claimed the next game is said to be *up.* Cf. *down, winners.* 3. To have the lead.

Up top (*prep* or *adv*) See *out front.*

Use (*v*) See *burn.*

Washington (*n*) See *change of hands.*

Wheeling and dealing (*v*) See *deal.*

Whirlybird (*n*) See *three-sixty.*

White Man's Disease (*n*) A grave illness, which prevents the afflicted from being able to jump.

Winners (*n*) 1. The system of inbounding that lets the scoring team retain possession of the ball after a basket. The ball is put back into play following a *check*. Encourages defensive play. Syn. *make it take it, possession*; cf. *losers*. 2. This is what a waiting player calls to claim rights to the next game—always to challenge the winning, defending team. Syn. *nexts*.

Yank (*n* or *v*) See *bound*.
You (*interj*) An exhortation one player will make to a teammate, to get him to take a shot or make a move.

Zebra (*n*) 1. A referee. 2. A player who thinks he's a ref and "calls" everything.
Zilch (*n*) See *zip*.
Zip (*n*) A score of zero. Syn. *zilch*.

Nicknames

If your feinting and movement have gotten you free for a fifteen-footer from the foul line, but your teammate has dribbled into the corner, has his back to you, and doesn't know that you're free, what can you do? You could call, "Hey foul line!" but it's much more personal to hail a teammate with a name. Full or formal names generally become contracted to single words or syllables in the playground's casual atmosphere. In fact, full names can be terribly cumbersome to pronounce in the split second you're open and want to get a teammate's attention. If your teammate happens to be cursed with a name like J. Parker Wallingford III, the defense will have recovered by the time you've uttered the last syllable. But a quick shout of "Park" or "Wall" or just "J" should serve your purpose. Let's face it: You rarely end up knowing the full names of everyone in a pick-up game. You end up using a first name, a last name, a variation on one of them, or a nickname.

A good nickname is succinct and, by connoting violence or grace, has some relation to the game. "Smitty" and "Red" and "Lefty" are hackneyed and unimaginative, and therefore should be reserved for football and baseball players. Some of the very best nicknames are coined almost by accident. Apparel with lettering or insignia is a good place to start looking for one, and it's frightening how apt these often are. If a player has been ignored while teams are being chosen, the captain who finally winds up taking him might resignedly say, "Awright, I got the guy in the green shorts." It's likely he'll be known as "Green Shorts" for the rest of the game. Or, if a player happens to be a member of the Spring Valley Athletic Club and his sweat shirt says so, the man who'll be guarding him might say, "I got SVAC." Or—this happens occasionally with ballplayers who attended Catholic grammar schools—"I got 'Our Lady.' " (Be careful, though, lest a nickname like this be construed derogatorily.)

Simple nicknames, too, can be daringly descriptive. Some players come packaged with brand names and commercial messages: "Velveeta" (" 'cause I'm so smooth") and "Windex" ("Gonna clean the glass, man"). "Pop" Green became known as such not for any willingness to shoot his jumper, but for a boyhood affinity for Rice Krispies. A New Jersey playground hanger-on never outlived an elementary school gym teacher's constant commands to "shape up" and is known as "Shape" today. Two of Shape's cronies are "Slop"—that's what people call the shots he throws up—and "Creeper," a deceptively savvy player who lulls opponents to sleep before making his move. And finally there's "Judge," who sits on the bench. Other nicknames are spin-offs of given family names: "Poison" Ivy, "Spider" Webb, "Hound" Baskerville, "Different" Drummer, "Mobile" Holmes, "Loony" Toone, and "Scratchy" Hines. (No one knows for sure whether Scratchy's middle initial is *B*.)

Names and nicknames of pro players can be bestowed on deserving playgrounders, though such usage should be selective. There are pro equivalents of just about every type of player. Here's a handy conversion table. Where two are given, use the representative with which you most closely identify:

QUALITY	PLAYER OR NICKNAME
Butcher	Toby Kimball, Dennis Awtrey
Yo-yo shooter	George McGinnis
Anything good	"Doctor"
Distance shooter	"Downtown" Freddie Brown
Bogarter	"Truck"
Sweet hook shot	"Kareem"
Left-handed white	Jack Marin, Kevin Grevey
Stonewall picks	Wes Unseld
Outlet passes	Bill Walton
Dazzling dribbler	Bob Cousy, Ernie "D"
High-arched jumper	"Rainbow"
From the hip	Jerry Lucas
Spin moves	"Pearl"
Double pump	"Greyhound"
Ambidexterity	Paul Westphal

White superstar	Larry Bird
Backboard-shattering jams	Gus Johnson, Darryl Dawkins*
Shot blocker	"Eraser"
Flashy passes	"Pistol," "Magic"
Never misses	"Iceman"

It may seem hard to believe, but no, Lloyd Free didn't wake up one morning and decide that anyone in his neighborhood who didn't call him "All-World" would get a slam-jam in his face. Long before Free got the reputation he has now, he was wowing the Brooklyn regulars with three-sixties. So they began to call him "Twirl," after what a globe does on its axis. The streets quickly transformed that into "Worl'," and, with Free's success, it eventually became "All-World."

Moses Malone claims he found the best comp in his hometown, Petersburg, Virginia, at "The Pen," the state penitentiary in Petersburg, where the best player was called "Milkman"—as Malone says, " 'cause he murdered a milkman, man."

One diminutive guard, said to be unstoppable one-on-one, is known only as "Napoleon Solo."

And a protégé of Harlem legend Earl Manigault had leaping ability so awe-inspiring Manigault anointed him "God."

---

* Someone once catalogued all fourteen of Darryl Dawkins' nicknames: Double D, Candy Slam, Dawk, Doctor Dunk, Sir Slam, Sweet D, Big Dawk, Squawkin' Dawkins, Double D Dunk, Sir Dunk, Dunk It, Pure Pleasure, Cool Breeze, and Zandhokan the Mad Dunker. If Darryl has anything to do with it, the list is still growing.

4. WHEN IN ROME

Violations

The schoolyard is an unpoliced world. So many of the standards of conventional basketball go unenforced that the lesser felonies become accepted, integral parts of the black-market game. The defender who doesn't hand-check out front is an exception. The player who has included a little foot shuffle in the pet move he's used since childhood isn't about to listen to a playground opponent who sees fit to "call" it. On the one hand, this is why so many coaches look upon the playground as a bane and breeding ground for bad habits. But at the same time it shows that pick-up ball is the sport's last bastion of *laissez-faire*. To get an idea of just how much is permitted in a typical schoolyard encounter, look at the following catalogue. It reads like a nullification of motherhood, apple pie, and anything else purists hold dear:

Goaltending, on city playgrounds at least, is never called. One Darwinian presumption predominates: If you can't adapt the trajectory of your shot to play with the big boys, you don't belong there.

Three-seconds isn't called either. On many courts, markings are faded or never existed, and the lane is a nebulous region. In anything other than a Five-on-Five contest, to call it would be silly, since the fewer players there are, the more the action tends to concentrate near the basket. The ability to post low, take a pass, and operate from there is a talent you want to reward, not penalize. (Still, anyone wanting to "claim residency" in the lane should be prepared to fill the residency requirement—taking a lot of pushing and bumping that can't really be called a foul.)

Palming and carrying aren't often called; if you get technical, almost every behind-the-back dribble is a carry, and banishing that would be unthinkable.

The heel-toe travel and step-before-dribbling are both tolerated, even sanctioned, by the asphalt game. Many players develop travels that become part and parcel of their moves. It's probably unfair to rob them of the foundation on which their "game" is based (though there are limits, such as the two-step, instead of one-and-a-half step, lay-up).

Exactly what does and doesn't constitute a foul is probably the

Laws of the asphalt jungle, codified

OPPOSITE PAGE:
If you want to "claim residency" be prepared to fill the residency requirement.

most enduring of schoolyard enigmas. Standards vary widely, according to such factors as who is playing, their individual styles and temperaments, and the prevailing style of the area. On one court it may be perfectly acceptable to holler "Foul!" if, after releasing the ball on a jump shot, your·shooting hand is met by a defender's slapping into it. Should the ball go in, you'll get the basket; if not, you'll be awarded the ball "up top" or "out front." But making exactly the same call somewhere else may bring a gallery of unfriendly grimaces to the faces of teammates and opponents alike. Someone may even say it: "What's with this white suburban fag foul?!" Be sure to learn the house code of conduct before making all but the most obvious calls on an unfamiliar court. Once you have some idea of what passes for a foul, you ought to be able to make your calls with a confidence that should avoid hassle. Generally, the higher the caliber of play, the more contact you'll have to endure before you can "call" it.

In an ideal game, fouls are called by the offender—that is, the defensive player. If the match isn't an intensely competitive one, and no individual cases of one-upmanship are playing themselves out, the honor system can be the most equitable. But it almost never works out that way; shooters usually have to stand up for themselves. And, in many games, someone will be timid about speaking up when fouled or, worse yet, mumble his protestation. All this does is slow things up, and sometimes adds an unnecessary tinge of antagonism to the atmosphere. If you're hesitant, not only is your call likely to be challenged but half the players won't hear you and will go right on playing. Messing up a good fast break with a whimper of self-pity won't help your bargaining position any, either, in case you want to file another complaint later on. Counting on the guilty party to fess up is risky for another reason; most streetwise ballplayers will expect you to do the talking and will take advantage of any uncertainty. The best policy: If you've been fouled, say so. Only you know what bludgeonings prevent you from playing your game.

Contact on the arm or hand during a shot—the foul all jump shooters love to call—is often ignored if the shooter has entered the lane. In other words, if you drive, don't expect the same protection you'll get if you stay outside.

Going "over the top" for a rebound is rarely called a foul per se; sometimes it's acknowledged, though, if neither player gains possession and the ball rolls out of bounds, by the offender giving up possession. The symptoms of lazy man's defense—bumping and

Shooting fingers, reminiscent of the Wild West, settles the score on city courts.

reaching in and around—are generally put up with, as are pushes and bumps away from the ball.

The offensive foul, too, is very rarely recognized, for several reasons. An impartial judge should call them, since a defender who is trying to draw one will think he has whether he *really* has or not. Most playground confrontations are a series of one-on-one match-ups taking place simultaneously, and helping teammates on defense—whence so many offensive fouls arise in refereed games—is not a high priority. Besides, aggressiveness is viewed as a premium.

For jump balls and other completely irresolvable incidents, you "shoot for it"—sometimes a basketball, sometimes fingers. If it's a basketball, the shot is taken from the foul line or beyond by the player who has made the call.

Shooting Fingers

Once, twice, drei, *shoot!*

When reason and argument fail to resolve a playground dispute, there's always the ultimate arbiter. "Shooting fingers" would seem to owe its origin to the Wild West. The principals face each other with fists cocked behind their backs, like loaded six-shooters. But they don't begin back to back and then whirl; instead they incant that Germanic-sounding countdown face to face. Just like pitching pennies and flipping baseball cards, it's an undeniable part of the playground culture.

"Shooting for it" means observing the following simple conventions: Each of two contestants—they are usually the two nearest where the ball went out, or the two tied up in a jump—sides with "odds" or "evens" and, on cue, presents any number of fingers. If the number of displayed fingers is an odd total, the "odds" contestant wins; if even, the "evens" contestant takes the ball out of bounds.

Shooting fingers evolved as it did for several reasons. There is no third party to toss up a jump ball in most pick-up games. As playgrounds boomed during the first half of the century, loose change was scarce, and in today's affluent times, athletic wear doesn't usually provide pockets. The result: Players often don't have a handy coin to flip. Going to the foul line and deciding who'll get possession there might be a method grounded in merit, but it's cumbersome and time-consuming.

Letting the numbers decide is the city's way of doing things. On small-town and rural courts, for instance, where shooting fingers is popular, the second questionable call to arise during a game is automatically resolved—by awarding the ball to the side that lost the first shoot-out. But in the city, where order finds it hard to gain a foothold, players won't go along with such a system, even if it's "fair." For every jump ball, one shoot-out. If one side takes all three or four in one game, the less fortunate team won't gripe. It's just as if someone else is rolling sevens in a crap game.

As simple as shooting fingers sounds, there can be complications. Among younger players especially there always seems to be some wise guy who sticks a fist out and taunts the trump, "Fistball beats 'em all." (Complete ostracism is the best way to deal with such puerile attention seekers.) Other hustlers have mastered the art of throwing a split second late and copping seemingly fair shoot-outs.

And as equitable as it sounds—could there be any more evenhanded means of awarding possession than letting fate, through numbers, do the choosing like tumbling dice?—there are ways to beat the fifty-fifty odds. Study the next handful of times people shoot fingers, and you'll notice the tendency is to shoot one finger. Keeping this in mind, let your opponent call "odds" or "evens" first, so that he doesn't suspect that you know as much as you do. Remember, you're expecting a "one." If you account for this when you throw your fingers—and consider, of course, whether you've been designated "odds" or "evens"—you should win close to 75 percent of the time. The other technique also relies on psychology, but could earn you a dubious reputation. (In other words, it's a bit dishonest.) When you face off, throw your fingers flagrantly late. Your opponent will almost certainly object and demand a reshoot. Make a note of the fingers he threw and apply this bit of reverse psychology: If he shot "one" the first time, he'll assume *you'll* think he's going to change it to "two" the next time. But, for that very reason, he won't. Expect a "one" again, and throw your fingers accordingly.

Make It Take It

"Make it take it" or "winners' out" applies in most urban school-yards for good reason: It provides a tremendous incentive to play defense in an environment that puts a premium on offense. After all, if you've just been burned and your opponent is getting the ball *right back again* . . . well, you, the burnee, are going to dig in just that much more. When "winners' out" *isn't* invoked on a city court, and two pick-up teams match flamboyance against flamboyance, there's likely to be plenty of showboating and not a lot of serious attention paid to the score. But the dictum of "if you score, you keep possession" immediately raises the possibility of a humiliating blowout, a defeat that would be short, decisive, and tough to swallow. Down three-, four-, or five-to-zip, a defender will be likely to rock from the heels to the balls of his feet.

By the same token, the whiter the half-court game, and the farther it is from the city's core, the more likely it'll be played according to "losers' out." Why should anyone, argue the devotees of "losers' out," *need* an incentive to play defense? What's more, some say, there's a sort of pleasurable condescension in handing the ball over to an opponent after just having administered a facial. ("Now let's see what you can do, sucker.")

Playing "losers' out" and deuce can be truly exhausting since, once you've reached "ad," you can't possibly have more than one opportunity in every two to score. But even the most passionate advocates of "winners' out" won't insist it be applied to the full-court run. No one wants to miss that exquisite grace period that comes when a team retreats in unison after having scored. On those few playgrounds where half-court ball is played either way, the format is decided upon before play starts, or the first team to score gets its preference.

Playground Lawyer's Casebook

Some playground lawyers have their own ideas about how to spend Saturday afternoons.

There are incidents that seem to raise questions—and tempers—time and time again during pick-up games. They invariably stop play and send asphalt attorneys into forensic fits. Knowing the proper solution to knotty problems as they come up can give you a

rep as a cool-headed parliamentarian, and should keep routine dis-
agreements from turning into full-scale litigation. Here are several
charges commonly brought by plaintiffs:

"The top and sides are out." A shot hits the top or side of the
backboard and bounces off the rim, returns to play, or falls
through the hoop. Some say both the top and sides are out; others
argue that the sides are in and the top is out. Still others maintain
that the top of rectangular boards is out, but the crest of fan
boards is in. But the rules state that the ball is *in play* unless it
touches the basket support or rear of the backboard, regardless of
backboard shape.

"You can't get a pass right after stepping inbounds." This line
usually comes from someone who claims that you've got to get
both feet back in bounds, and that someone else must touch the
ball, before you can touch it again after going out. Address this ig-
noramus with a clear throat and the manner of F. Lee Bailey: You
not only can come directly back in bounds and immediately receive a pass, but there's also no need for anyone else to touch the
ball first. The rules only forbid reentering the court at a "more ad-
vantageous position." (Use that phrase exactly and no one will
doubt that the rule book can back you up.)

"Hand's part of the ball." Everyone's heard this expression, and
everyone uses it . . . but what does it mean? Some will invoke it as
a rationale for striking the hand of a shooter, which is incorrect.
"Hand's part of the ball" should always be interpreted so as not to
give an advantage to the defender, but to protect the offensive
player. The hand *is* considered part of the ball when a defender
slaps the hand of an offensive player who is holding the ball, or
when such action knocks it out of bounds. In the first instance, no
foul is called; in the second, possession remains with the offense.

"No harm, no foul." Another oft-heard lyric. With ten people
moving up and down a court, there's bound to be some contact. If
it's incidental to play, it isn't cause for a foul. "No harm, no foul"
doesn't mean that anything short of bloodshed is acceptable. Still,
it's reasonable to expect more contact in a pick-up game than in a
professionally officiated contest. Degree of contact is a judgment—*your* judgment. If you feel you've been unfairly hacked,
call your foul loud and clear.

"You called it—no basket." There are some playgrounds—in
particular those that look down on chronic foul-callers and want
to curb stops in play—where if you call a foul on your shot, the
basket won't count even if it goes in. These spots are rare, but if
you're playing at one, you'd best think twice before calling any-

thing on your shot. On most playgrounds, a shooter's foul call will be ignored if the shot drops, and the score will be duly registered. Where you'll get yourself into an uncomfortable situation is in making a late call on incidental contact, after the "statute of limitations" has expired. Whether your tardiness is calculated or accidental, you'll be viewed as an opportunist trying to have it both ways: If the ball had gone in, you'd get the basket; if it hadn't, you'd get it back with a foul call. You won't be disbarred for trying to finagle your way through this loophole, but you may get yourself into trouble by trying it on the wrong people.

Official basketball rules leave referees with a great deal of leeway for making judgment calls. If you elect to become a playground lawyer, it can't hurt to know your rules, even to the point of reciting chapter and verse. If you don't know them, you can always fake it, claiming you ref high school games during the winter. If you're convincing, chances are no one will call your bluff. But one thing you should never catch yourself doing is bringing the rule book to the park. You'll alienate everyone. Commit these cases—and any others that seem to keep cropping up—to memory.

OPPOSITE PAGE:
"Hand's part of the ball,"
and this block is a clean
one.

5. THE POLITICS OF PICK-UP BALL

And those whose names were never called
When choosing sides for basketball.
> —Janis Ian

Can't dunk? No one need know until after the game begins

Maybe you have a rep and carry personal rebounders from playground to playground the way Ali took along sparring partners. Crowds in schoolyards part like the Red Sea as soon as you enter the fenced-in compound. And claims to "winners" are quickly forgotten as everyone scrambles to be on your team. But for most of us, being a "face man" before a game begins is the best way to get a chance to be an in-your-face man once it starts. In other words, you don't have to be good to get on a good pick-up team; the key is being street-smart and making a good impression.

It starts with your appearance. Black socks simply won't do. When you join the geriatric set in Miami Beach, it'll be perfectly acceptable to wear black socks with shorts and sneakers, but for now, never, ever wear them to the playground. Leave at home those $2.99 Red Ball made-in-Japan sneakers you found loose in metal wire barrels in the supermarket; wearing them on the asphalt is like tap dancing in moon boots. Real basketball players wear serious sneakers, so get some. And that doesn't mean tennis shoes, which are a dead giveaway that you're nothing more than a once-a-year player. Leave your tennis pumps at home, and discreetly suggest to anyone who does play in them that they've stumbled upon the wrong court. By wearing at least two pairs of socks, you'll not only do your feet a favor, but show that you're serious about your game. And a sweatband doesn't hurt either. Your shirt can be of the sleeveless, "T," or sweat variety, but don't wear a button-down, long-sleeved shirt. Unless you already have a rep, you'll be viewed at best as having a severe case of cooties, and when captains choose teams, they'll steer clear.

Then there are the basics of racial etiquette; if you're not aware of them, you can blunder your way off of a good team. If you're white, you don't have to have read *Soul on Ice* or even *Black Like Me* to mingle on the darker playgrounds. Just take care to exhibit at least a modicum of cultural cosmopolitanism. Do not, for instance, do what Kevin Grevey did once in a game of H-O-R-S-E.

Playing against Bingo Smith, Grevey made a shot that involved bouncing the ball off the top of his head. Smith, charged with duplicating it, was irked. "Gonna mess up my 'fro, man," he said. By the same token, it would be ethnocentric for a player whose hair is set in corn rows to expect a white opponent to make a shot that involved rolling the ball along the top of his head. On such minor misunderstandings racial tension thrives.

Whites in search of good hoop action on foreign turf should avoid the obvious pitfalls. Don't bandy funky phrases about, thinking they will endear you to the playground populace. Offering an unsolicited explanation on how you believe affirmative action is necessary to achieve a truly integrated society won't help you either. On the other hand, don't be completely insensitive to race, and don't act as though, if you handled the Coppertone ac-

People notice when a guy with a rep struts through the fence.

Checking out the comp at a new park, before breaking a sweat.

count for some ad agency, you'd try to contract a full page in *Ebony*. Everyday common sense and normal discretion should keep you from committing these faux pas. Once the game gets under way, just keep quiet and play the strongest, savviest brand of ball you can. Also, make sure you're not the first to throw an elbow. (But if someone tests your testosterone by giving you one, return it to show you're no pushover.) And don't try to change your style to match the fashion prevailing at a more soulful schoolyard; if you were brought up on a gospel that revered the twenty-foot set shot, don't blaspheme it by heading for the hoop with an array of off-balance, scooped double pumps. You'll be appreciated for what you can contribute, not what you can't.

If you're the only black on a white playground, there's no need to come off "super cool." You're likely to be chosen for a team immediately. Opponents will warn each other to "box out" and "guard the baseline" on you since, moves unseen, you're probably "a great leaper" or at least "quick" (though, alas, never a "pure shooter"). Others may surmise you've just had a couple of bad games at a black playground and, in shame, have retreated to this one to get your confidence back. If you put stock in such stereotyped reactions, you may think whites will consider you an expert of sorts. But beware: Whites, once universally flattered by a black player in their midst and almost childlike in their desire to soak up some of the Afro-American kharma, are becoming more assertive. Still, you can parlay selective compliments into the kind of guilt feelings that will send the ball your way more often. A few headlong dives for loose balls never fail to impress. And one buttering-up technique is well known and widely used: Whites love it when blacks call them by the name of a white pro star. After some tow-headed kid with glasses rolls in a lame ten-footer from the baseline, shout, "Havlicek from eighteen!" You'll have won his everlasting devotion. If he should respond by grinning at you, clenching his right fist, and saying, "Right on, bro'!" be indulgent. He means well.

While keeping these subtleties of racial politics in mind, be sure you go through your warm-ups scientifically. Get several unorthodox shots down pat, so you can run through them nonchalantly. Casual finger rolls and carefree double pumps are perfect for this purpose. If you sink them, everyone will be impressed; if you don't, be sure to mutter "Damn!" after each miss, as if you normally make them but today some inexplicable force is playing havoc with your pet shots. It may be worthwhile to stop by the local candy store on your way to the park. Buy a candy bar for any kid hanging out there who promises to come by the court while you're warming up to ask for your autograph. Also, honor with lavish "courtesy" everyone who sinks a shot during warm-ups. Not only will this buy you some time if you don't happen to be on your game, but it may get you a quick reputation as the playground's philanthropist. When teams are finally chosen, the more talented players, thinking that you enjoy being a feeder, will be likely to snap you up.

But if teams are formed according to who sinks foul shots— usually the first five to hit make up one team—neither flattery, posturing, nor sequin-studded tube socks will give you an edge. Work on that free throw, and choose a spot toward the end of the shooting line. As one team begins to load up with strong players, keep this team in mind when *you* shoot. Then make or miss your shot accordingly. But be sure any intentionally missed free throws are short or long; off to one side looks suspicious.

If the playground is fairly full, the foul-shooting method for picking teams will defer to the "winners" system, where a waiting player calls "winners" or "nexts." (Some well-managed parks even have sign-up sheets on which players register for "nexts.") If it doesn't appear that you'll be able to get on the first or even the second team to form, don't panic or anxiously inquire who has "winners." Be cool, loosen up, and use the time to cultivate your image. Get in those effortless hooks and spins while play has stampeded to the far end of the court. If your show is convincing, whoever is "down" should proffer an invitation soon enough.

Even if your talent isn't so awesome that it sends team captains into swoons as soon as you cock your wrist, you can ride the coattails of a bona fide hotshot onto a good team. Just project the image of being inseparable from a local star and you'll soon hear captains saying, "I got Ace and his partner." It certainly helps if

"Don't tell me you're looking for some badder dude!": It seems everybody is his own best salesman when you're forced to pick a fifth.

Gone are the days when guys would only let girls play if they went "skins."

your buddy with the rep is willing to chirp up paternalistically on your behalf as teams form. Several finely executed give-and-gos during warm-ups may plant the idea in someone's head that you're part of a tandem. Hanging out together helps, too, as does arriving at and departing from the playground as a unit.

If you're a girl, just getting on a court can be a challenge. You may have to bolt down your dinner so you can get to the playground early in the evening, before any guys do. (It's a lot easier for guys to refuse to admit you to a game already in progress than it is for them to muster the cruelty to run you off.) Happily, the days are over when guys would let you on a team only if you played "skins." Now if you end up in a game with men, you may find them respectful, and almost cavalierly unwilling to block your shot—should they get the chance. It seems that, more and more, women in co-ed games are the ones that have to restrain themselves so that no one gets embarrassed.

Lady or gentleman, once you're on a team, don't jeopardize your standing with a socially inept breach of pick-up etiquette. For instance, there is a justified, long-standing taboo on substituting while a game is in progress. It's unfair; a team getting a fresh player is likely to be strengthened. But more than that, the "pride thing" dictates that, once a game ends, both winners and losers realize exactly who has triumphed and who has been vanquished. Pick-up games are personal encounters, and shuttling men *or* women in and out reduces the keenness and intimacy of competition.

If you end up a winner, just what are you entitled to? First and foremost, you can keep the court, which means your team is guaranteed the next game, and as many games thereafter, as long as you can win. Beyond that, you've got to negotiate for additional privileges. You'll normally be allowed to begin the next game with possession of the ball; announce your prerogative in the vernacular, to make sure everyone knows you'll "bring it up." You may want to change the basket you're shooting at, to avoid a low sun or

Recruiting the prima donna can be difficult but rewarding.

skewed hoop. Or you may opt for "shirts" (if the sun has been merciless during the last run) or "skins" (if you want to see how many hearts you can break with that hirsute chest of yours). You should be able to make a strong case for any of these perks if your team holds court; try trading off those less dear for ones you really want. Remember that challengers have the right to start the next game immediately.

If there's only one ball among fifteen people and it happens to be yours, you're more or less guaranteed a spot on one of the two

Crucial to forming a good pick-up team is avoiding the chumps.

teams to form if you really want it. Of course, it's always best if you don't have to threaten; everyone will view someone who poses an ultimatum like, "If you don't let me play, I'm taking my ball home" as infantile at best. But you can make a good case for nominating yourself as captain if you provide the ball. (Don't, however, assume you can stay on if you lose a game and another group has "winners." And insisting that you "gotta go"—and take your rock with you—is sure to alienate everyone if yours is the only available ball.)

If you don't have a rep, and certainly if you don't have a ballplayer's body, merely calling "winners" may not guarantee anything. Many playground regulars remain unimpressed by mediocre-appearing strangers who happen by and put themselves down for the next game. Aggressively defend your claim to the game; don't sit idly around, thinking that calling "winners" is some sacred self-anointment. It helps to immediately enlist a regular for your squad, as a sort of imprimatur. What's more, he should be able to advise you on who to tab for the rest of your team. If you're doing the choosing and you're a regular, you ought to have a decent idea of who can play. But if you're not familiar with the crowd at this particular playground and no one nearby seems willing to advise you, here are a few tips for choosing a good team:

Go for speed. Lumbering, methodical players are less effective on the playgound than in organized ball. Fast, open court players—especially if you're running full—can usually get you to game point in a hurry. They won't be inclined to waste time setting up plays (when there's really nothing to set up), and they're quick enough to get back on D and prevent a game from degenerating into a sloppy, lay-up for lay-up affair. Teams composed of one lazy, slow rebounder and outlet passer and four speed merchants have been known to hold court for hours.

Learn how to recruit. There are sometimes reluctant prima donnas, players with egos to match their skills, who come to the park with their own balls, shoot lazily on side baskets, and only half expect to run. If you try to induce them to play, they turn you down with some lame excuse like, "I don't feel like runnin' today," when all the while they're just waiting for comp to come by that they feel is worth breaking a sweat over. If you can bring yourself to it, try to woo them with flattery.

Be an equal opportunity employer. You don't have to come up with the kind of squad the guy who did the casting for *Room 222* might have picked, but strive for a good racial balance nonetheless. As one black player says: "When you get five brothers together, each one's out for himself. With four blacks and one white—you know, a busted flush—the white usually gets ignored. But three brothers and two whites is the perfect mix, especially if one of the white dudes handles the ball. The team's still funky, but the whites keep it from getting too wild."

Avoid chumps. Crucial to forming a good pick-up team is *avoiding* getting together a bad one. If you've got "winners" and some 5'3" overweight chump waddles over wanting to get into the next game, try a diplomatic tack first. A general manager's spiel, something like "We've got three backcourt types already and we're looking for a power forward," should get the message across. If not, be brutal but straight: "Look, you're a chump, and I don't think you're gonna help any, and I don't want to sit after one run. Why don't you go home and listen to some Janis Ian?"

6. FORBIDDEN FUNDAMENTALS

To BE the "complete player" these days, you're expected to be able to perform a lot more than just the two-handed chest pass and crossover dribble. The new flamboyance isn't all just for appearances, either; certain skills are guerrilla tactics essential for doing battle in the asphalt jungle. So the next time an old schooler gets on your case for what he calls "a poor percentage shot," answer with a slam dunk. (There's nothing quite as high percentage as that.) For everyone whose coach ever dealt out twenty-lap penalties for throwing a behind-the-back pass:

No coach ever told you about these

The Slam Dunk

Ah, the slam dunk! It's the most dramatic and satisfying shot in the game, and every runt in the world wants to know what it's like. Well, the similes run the gamut from the succulently gastronomic ("Like lifting out the first scoop of fresh Jell-O") to the perversely political ("Like exercising the cruelty and power of Idi Amin"). And its power is tonic. As Lloyd Hill, a Brooklyn playground player, told author Rick Telander in *Heaven Is a Playground*: "I think I may put my bed out under that basket, sleep right there, and take a few jams when I get up in the morning." One shot and you're good for the whole day. . . .

Within the genus *dunk* there are two species: *punk dunk* and *funk dunk*. Neither has as its primary purpose scoring points. The punk dunk is expressly for occasions where face is at stake, where the object is the utter humiliation of the defender. (This, since in the dunking arms race the defense is light-years behind the offense, is fairly easily done.) The funk dunk, on the other hand, is an improvisation: The dunker is a saxophone player, soaring and jamming, trying to hit all the notes that will express his feelings before his allotted beats are up. The prerequisite to dunking is, of course,

TANK M^cNAMARA

Copyright © 1977 Universal Press Syndicate. Used by permission.

enormous talent and leaping ability, which could be the reason jamming technique isn't covered in basketball primers. But don't be deceived. There are certain aerodynamic principles, yes, even fundamentals, you ought to get down before you *can* "get down"—properly, safely, and consistently. After all, a missed dunk halts momentum more effectively than a spate of airballs. Some simple rules:

1. If you can't jam it home with one hand, don't bother trying with two.

2. Carefully get your approach steps down. You should treat them with the same seriousness a high jumper would.

3. Keep your hands as dry as possible. Many missed dunks stem from clammy hands.

4. Don't extend too much of your arm over the rim. If you're a marginal dunker, you won't get the downward flick of the wrist necessary for a crisp, clean dunk unless you get enough vertical spring off your approach. Too much arm indicates an overly horizontal approach, which often results in a "rub-in," a successful dunk that fudges around the rim. Getting adrenaline out of that is like getting water from a coin.

Some of the infinite varieties of slam dunk, with notes on their practitioners, performance, and aesthetic value:

The Afterthought. George Gervin's pet. Pascal and Rodin would have loved to be able to do this one. Both vertical and horizontal movement—that is, hang time—are crucial. You take off even with either baseline, float past the rim while contemplating some metaphysical problem, and in a sudden vengeance jackknife the baggage back through the twine. A dunk of passion.

The Bank. Scoop the ball lightly, high off the glass, as you come

OPPOSITE PAGE:
Just about any runt can get satisfaction at eight feet.

in from the foul line; then leap up and send it home. The After-thought Bank is a bit more of a challenge: Lay it off the glass on one side of the hoop, scoot under, leap, and jackknife it in from the other side.

The Circle. A Darrell Griffith specialty. The dunker palms the ball at takeoff, waves it in a broad, circumscribed motion perpendicular to the ground, and rams it in.

The Corkscrew, Three-Sixty, or Goat. The body makes one full revolution before jamming. The performer should have the body control of an Olympic diver, though the movement is upward into O_2 rather than downard into H_2O. Usually resolved with a two-handed flourish.

The Cradle-the-Baby. Clutch the ball to your body in one arm, as high up as is necessary. Then leap, making sure the ball is suspended over the rim, and at that instant bang it in with your free fist. An unquestionable funk dunk, dedicated to mothers everywhere.

The Cuff. The ball is wedged against the wrist, between the forearm and palm. The trick to this is preparing for it late enough so you don't travel, and soon enough to finish it off.

Dawkinsian Dunk. Darryl Dawkins has spawned almost as many varieties of personalized dunk as he has nicknames. Aside from the vaunted Go-rilla, described below, there is the Left-handed Spine-Chiller Supreme, the Sexophonic Turbo Delight, the Earthquake Breaker, the Flop-a-Dop, the Look Out Below, the Dunk You Very Much, the Hammer of Thor, the One We Owe You, and the No Playin' Get Out of the Wayin' Backboard Swayin' Game Delayin'. To cope with many of these, someone has invented a collapsible rim with a magnetic bracket that attaches the basket to the backboard. With sufficient force, the hoop flops harmlessly down, and can be flipped back into place.

There'll soon be one in every arena in the NBA, if the Dawk's Chocolate Thunder Flying, Robinzine Crying, Teeth Shaking, Glass Breaking, Rump Roasting, Bun Toasting, Wham Bam, Glass Breaker I Am Jam is any indication of where pro basketball's arms race is headed. (Dawkins gusjohnsoned that ornately named dunk in the collective faces of Bill Robinzine and the Kansas Cuty Kings, and came up with a similar number a few weeks later.)

The Double Dip. You won't find this one in the vanilla bin at Baskin-Robbins. It's a combination of the dunk and the double pump. In one leap, the ball is dunked, retrieved, and dunked again. Al McGuire says, "They ought to award four points for it."

The Go-rilla. The Dawk is the only creature with the physical dimensions that can really do this shot justice. The basket is usually approached from the front for this two-handed number, which is marked by the height and extension of both elbows and the ferocity of the throwdown.

The Grab 'n' Jab. Grab the rim with one hand, jab the ball through with the other.

The Hook. Sweep a broad swath with your shooting hand, just as if you were letting go a hook shot, only bring the ball down to the rim instead of letting it go early. A resolute downward flick of the wrist should keep the ball from rattling against both sides of the rim and bounding out.

The Midwife. Approach from any angle and take off while palming the ball. In midair, lift up your shirt with your free hand, stick the ball underneath, and "deliver" it—back out again and into the hoop. Suggested attire: a loose-fitting T-shirt.

The Mister Clean. You'll need a good leap and complete arm

LEFT:
The Reverse: By necessity a two-hander.

RIGHT:
Darryl Dawkins' alma mater, the Ivey Lane Elementary School in Orlando. This is the planet Lovetron. Zandhokan, the Mad Dunker, stalks its surface, leaving rims vertical in his path.

If you can block your man out, it helps, but don't be overly concerned with it. Find the ball with one hand and bring it down suddenly.

extension for this one, a straight dunk—usually two-handed—in which neither your hand, wrist, arm, nor the ball touch rim or backboard. The "swoosh" you'll hear will be louder than the "swish" you're accustomed to.

The Reverse. A "sense of where you are" job, with back to the basket. By necessity a two-hander, and it can be as devastating as the Go-rilla.

The Rocking Chair. As you'd expect, this starts from a stand-still. Position yourself under or right next to the basket, grip the ball with two hands, swing it up from your knees and over your head as you jump, and rock it forward, through the hoop.

The Tap. The smaller you are, the more dramatic this one—an explosive punk dunk—is. During a game it's essentially a tip-in, only the ball is escorted door to door, from hand to basket. As a floor exercise—sometimes called the Bounce Dunk—bounce the ball high off the asphalt, leap up, and do it. Guaranteed to get at least 9.5's from the Eastern European judges.

The Yo-Yo. The ball is pumped back and forth behind the head twice before being violently disposed of.

Slap the ball resolutely with your free hand as you return to earth.

Rebounding Ruthlessly (but with flair)

In pick-up ball, rebounding is essential. With most games played according to "make it take it," and if you assume both sides will play errorless ball, the only time possession will change hands is with a rebound. But just because rebounding is important doesn't mean it has to be drab and dull, as it often is. Most prospective bounders establish "position," expose their armpits, and, well, "get" rebounds.

There's a more exciting way to snag a defensive bound:

1. Get near the spot to which you think the carom will come. If you can block your man out, it helps, but don't be overly concerned with it. You're looking for air space, not "position."

2. Find the ball with one hand and bring it down suddenly, while lewdly spread-eagling your legs and letting go a simian, foreboding grunt.

3. Complete your percussive solo by slapping the ball resolutely with your free hand as you return to earth. (By now, the ball should be down below your waist, in heretical disregard of basketball textbooks.)

Before any grounded players get a notion to dig at the ball, stick your elbows out and pivot.

4. Before any grounded players get a notion to dig at the ball, stick your elbows out menacingly and pivot around in a complete circle. "Executing a pull" isn't quite the same as "getting a rebound," eh?

Shooting on the Way Down

Leapers whose aerial displays seem to cast Isaac Newton as an academic fraud are really masters of the art of shooting on the way down. It takes both strength and concentration to sink, for instance, a double pump. Coaches tend to call shots of this variety "forces." But if they've been practiced, and aren't launched from Outer Mongolia, there's no reason why they can't become a valuable—and fairly high percentage—part of any shooter's repertoire.

The Fallaway. The most useful variety of shots *en descendant*, and the most widely accepted type in conservative cage circles, though some basketball pedants object to it on the ground that the shooter can't follow his shot. The key is to be square to the basket, keep your eyes fixed on the hoop, and have your shooting hand end up looking like a cobra head.

The Up-and-Under. A lay-up for which the shooter approaches the basket from a sharp angle, shows the ball to the near side of the rim, tucks it while floating underneath, and lays it up backward. By putting gobs of spin on the ball and letting the backboard redirect it, you can make this shot seem almost effortless. In traffic, its difficulty factor redoubles.

The Whirlybird. Brooklyn legend Fly Williams' specialty, this is the Corkscrew Dunk's approach without the high-percentage finish. Consequently, the shooter only gets a last-second glimpse of the hoop. Again, in a crowd, much harder.

Alley-Oop

The alley-oop is that classic establishment play, the backdoor, raised to a higher plane. Players don't really learn how to execute this move; it's more as though the alley-oop selectively allows sufficiently talented duos to become practitioners of its arcane art. You need one passer and one leaper. The passer signals the leaper with a gesture or knowing look, and lobs a pass just to one side and at or above the level of the rim; the leaper responds by skying, grabbing, and jamming. Timing is crucial, as is the placement of the pass.

On the Up-and-Under, apply gobs of spin and a prayer.

The No-Backboard Lay-up

For those who can only dunk with a volleyball, this is the next best thing. (And those who *can* jam should do as Wilt Chamberlain did in developing a finger roll: Exercise occasional restraint.) Most coaches abhor the boardless lay-up and implore their players to use the backboard. But the board is an intermediary, and why use it if it's not necessary? Commune directly with the net. A swished lay-up can be every bit as satisfying as a twenty-foot twine-twinkler. The approach differs slightly from that of a conventional lay-up. You don't need a banking angle, so you should move toward the basket, not the backboard. From there, all the canned lay-up advice applies: Take off from the foot opposite the hand you're shooting with, extend your arm fully, and concentrate on your target. That target, remember, is the inside of the net. Coaches object to this shot primarily because the ball can easily kick off the back of the rim if it's not dropped just right. Lift your arm with the back of your hand facing the net—but be wary of chain nets.

Showboat Dribbles

The through-the-legs dribble is the schoolyard's substitute for the crossover. It allows you to change hands without having the ball dangerously—and drably—out in front of you. The first leg the ball goes under should be the one on the ball side, while that leg is striding forward; the leg provides protection from defenders, and isn't likely to impede the ball's clean passage from right hand to left. (How many would-be dribbling wizards have you seen try this move and ineptly send the ball off a fat hip or poorly positioned heel?)

The behind-the-back dribble is more practical, and allows for a longer stride and better protection of the ball than the crossover. Two important points, though: Don't let your body lag behind the ball, or you'll fudge up the passage from one side to the other (or worse, flagrantly carry to avoid doing so); also, watch with your peripheral vision the spot the ball should reach when the move is complete and it's time to resume normal dribbling.

Behind-the-Back Pass

Long a forbidden fruit dangled in front of generations of guards, the behind-the-back pass has recently acquired a measure of respectability. Still, most coaches haven't yet given in; as a result the

OPPOSITE PAGE:
The No-Backboard Lay-Up: Commune directly with the net.

Compared to the drab crossover, the through-the-legs dribble is a flashier way to switch hands.

move remains sweet to use in pick-up games. It's deceptively difficult, however, and hardest off the break and with the weak hand. A valuable drill involves whipping the ball behind your back against a designated spot on a solid wall. Try it from a standstill first, then while moving, and don't let the fact that the pass is now treated in ball-handling lectures at basketball clinics discourage you.

Spin Move

This maneuver, often called a "whirl" or "pearl," involves committing the unforgivable sin of turning your back on your opponent. (But so what? Is it rude? If you execute the spin move properly, you won't see him for a while anyway.) Plant the foot *opposite* the side on which you're dribbling; then turn your body, quickly, so you lose sight of the basket, all the while pulling at the ball with your dribbling hand. As you come out of the spin, take a big step with your nonpivot foot, and you should break away with ease.

Cherry Picking

You know those leeches: Moments after a shot's gone up and four guys are busting their rears on the boards, they're playing Lynn Swann and yelling "send it." But instead of griping about cherry pickers, why not become one? Selectivity is the key. By picking your spots and not abusing the privilege, you can cherry pick, snowbird, or basket-hang without suffering either the derision of opponents or the ostracism of more Calvinistic teammates. It's best to head for the orchard when your team is ahead. In the meantime, at least give the appearance of trotting back to play D, and by all means don't linger at center court when your man is handling the ball on offense.

Lazy Man's Defense

Let's face it—if you'll pardon the pun. There's only so much satisfaction you can get out of playing defense in a pick-up game. Quite often your teammates think "de-fense" is what goes around the house—a chronic attitude that spawned the "winners" system

Blocking a shot on the way down: Try tipping the ball from the side.

of inbounding—and many players hope to get by with a minimum of D in order to save their energy for a circus shot. So here's how to pick up several snuffs and steals without prematurely calling for a water break:

Blocking a Shot on the Way Down. Everyone is a foil for a Chet Walker fake, a head and shoulders juke that gets any defender with even the remotest notion of blocking a shot airborne. (In fact, it may be a little complicity of the playground world that the defender so willingly goes for this fake because he expects his opposite number to reciprocate when the roles are switched.) To stop a shot as you're falling, *after* you've left your athletic supporter down around your ankles, swing your weak hand around, and try to tip the ball from the side as your opponent lets go.

Reach-around Steal. Quite often this results from a last-ditch effort. You've been caught flat-footed, and an instant later your man will be by you for two. Rather than employing the Matador Defense and waving as he goes by, take a tip from the guy on the other side of the fence who's losing big at craps and throws out everything he has to recoup his losses: If your man has beaten you on your right, pivot quickly on your right foot and jab at the ball from behind with your left hand. (Your opponent should be dribbling with his left hand.) If he beats you to your left, simply reverse the move. Only referees call "reaching in." If you tip the ball loose and it goes out of bounds or, better yet, a teammate grabs it, you've done your job.

Palmistry

The ability to palm the ball is necessary for the crisp execution of most dunks, but it's a skill that can be used in many other facets of the game, too. Connie Hawkins began doing it so he'd have a free hand with which to ward off defenders. And the vicious bound, the outlet pass, the post play—all are aesthetically improved if you can manhandle and yo-yo the ball. Those who don't have suction cups for fingertips may have to wait for a light rain to coat the ball before they can palm it. So if you've got some George McGinnisian move up your sleeve, but you can't seem to pull it off, save it for a rainy day.

Spinning the Ball

Spinning the ball won't help you much once a game is under way, but it could impress someone beforehand if you're hoping to latch

Spinning the ball, though not much use in a game, can impress people before one.

on to a team. It doesn't matter with which spot on the ball's surface your finger makes contact, as long as it's at the bottom of the globe. It also doesn't matter in which direction the ball spins. Just be sure to keep your fingernails short, and remember how important that first twist of spin is. Until you've perfected the technique of slapping the side of the ball—Hap Hairston did it well in that beer commercial—it will fall off after the first dosage of spin is used up.

Crowd Pleasing

There aren't always throngs of spectators at pick-up games, but when there are, it's worth catering to them. If you keep leaving a distinct impression on a crowd, your rep will eventually reap the benefits. And there's a more immediate payoff for crowd pleasing: Once you reach game point, an audience that's been entertained will return the favor—by coaxing out the adrenaline that lets you cop the contest.

Keep in mind the ·difference between crowd pleasing and hot-dogging, however. Ostentatious and obnoxious behavior is going to backfire on you. Don't crassly bait your opponent or stick your fist in the air after a sweet "J." Still, a certain amount of cockiness is not only in order, it's what distinguishes the schoolyard player. Dress smartly. Strut, don't walk. On two-on-oh breaks, don't always sail in for the score yourself; give the ball to your teammate once in a while—with a behind-the-back pass. Quarterback the defense. Smile from time to time. Drop little asides, "just between us," to the crowd. Remember that nothing delights them more than a big talker who can back up what he says. Ruthian "called shots" are the stuff of which legends are made; just ask Harlem's "Rabbit" Walthour. While playing once in a full-court grudge match, with the booty—everyone's watches—heaped in a pile on the sidelines, Walthour had the ball at game point. From midcourt he yelled, "For the watches!" and threw in a forty-foot hook shot.

7. COPING WITH THE TEN-FOOT CULTURE

BASKETBALL is as loose as the rims on many inner-city courts, and the playground variety is the sport at its freest. Given all the variables—in rim height and condition, net state, backboard composition, court surface, and weather—there's an almost infinite variety of outdoor courts. The result is the richness of the outdoor game. Luck is the residue of design, it's been said, so don't attribute completely to fortune that corner jumper that hits the top of the backboard and falls through. Darwin's law holds: The team that can adapt to an inconveniently positioned sun, or a crater of a pothole, is going to prevail. Players learn to cope, and teams of copers end up winning.

When the basket is 10'2"

The Ball

The basketball is normal enough. Clean-cut and healthy, it's not unshaven like a tennis ball, leprous like a soccer ball, or deformed like a football. Oh, there are fancy leather ones designed for indoor play and colorful rubber-coated spheres for outdoor use. But the basketball isn't much more than a globe that, when in good hands, can be induced into doing some pretty impressive things.

If you use a leather ball outdoors, the cover will wear down until only a slick, graying hide remains. If put to additional outdoor abuse, the ball will soon reveal the black bladder of the inner tube. At today's prices, buying a leather ball for outdoor use is probably the quickest way to show off your ignorance. (On an outdoor court, you can be sure the guy who prefers a leather ball—or has in fact brought one—is either a habitual indoor player or independently wealthy, so take advantage of his lack of familiarity with the elements or well-heeled prissiness.)

Rubber balls aren't constructed with the care of their leather kin. They come in odd sizes and with varying surface textures. Some are too small; others too big. Some are too heavy; others too light. Some are too slippery; still others too sticky. None, it's easy to convince yourself, is just right. The variety of rubber balls adds to the adventure of playing outdoors. While an old, worn ball ought to be respected for its age, getting a grip on one is nearly impossible. Brand-new rubber balls, on the other hand, are spheri-

The basketball isn't much more than a globe that, when in good hands, can be induced into doing some pretty impressive things.

cal invitations to play "Doctor," they are so easily palmed. Many will eventually develop cysts, which, when coupled with bald spots, signal the time for retirement. But if that rubber ball is plastic-coated, different rules apply: An old plastic-coated rubber ball is easier to grip than a new one, which is generally slick and slippery.

If you have a nostalgic bent, you'll not want to pass up a game in which a red, white, and blue ball is used. Despite the abuse aficionados of this motley missile must endure—"With that and a towel you can go to the beach" and "Only defunct players use balls from defunct leagues" are commonly heard taunts—this ABA relic gives the shooter a chance to see the backspin on his shot and quickly troubleshoot a bad habit. Sure, the traditionalists will urge its ouster from the game, and will offer a standard orange number in its place, but keep them at bay. You owe it to the game's history. And by all means throw up a few twenty-five-footers in honor of the three-point field goal, which was pioneered with the ABA ball.

If you own a ball, be sure it's marked before you bring it to the playground. This may not be so simple; rain and dirt, along with constant pounding on asphalt, will probably erode efforts to maintain your own autographed ball. If you're not willing to re-mark yours every few months, your best bet is to study it closely and memorize its idiosyncrasies. Look for a little nick in the seam or an incipient cyst. Examine the condition around the air-intake valve. And identify any discoloration, too, all the while keeping in mind that showing up on a crowded playground with your own ball means that, for the next few hours, it will be viewed as community property.

Sneaking into Gyms

One thing Abbie Hoffman forgot to include in *Steal This Book*, his classic of the counterculture, was a definitive chapter on sneaking into gyms. The biggest problem with indoor playgrounds is their exclusivity: You have to either belong or pay in order to play. But rather than joining up or shelling out, the hard-core playgrounder should learn to cope. Case out the spot thoroughly before deciding on which of the following techniques to apply. Finding an insider who's familiar with layout, hours, and customs can make the job run more smoothly. If the first method of attack should fail, try another . . . and if you get caught, be sure to act self-righteously.

The ABA ball: Though some call it a "beach ball," it's always good for an occasional 25-footer.

The Inside Job. Find a sympathetic janitor or nightwatchman who will let you in at a designated time. This method has the added advantage of unofficial sanction: You can play without worrying about being discovered and booted out (don't games always seem to get cut short when they're grudge matches that have worked themselves to "deuce"?), and your accomplice is likely to know how the gym lighting works. *Really* sympathetic maintenance workers may even loan you the key. If you can't find an insider and you're dedicated enough, check the job listings and see if you can't become one yourself. As soon as you've duplicated the keys, feel free to quit the job.

The ID Card Glide. If you know a member of, or student at, an institution with a gym, have him report his ID card lost and then pocket the extra he's issued. Often it'll be an interim card without a photo on it, which is best over the short term. But even with a photo—and a historic expiration date—strategic thumb and index-finger positioning along with a preoccupied gait should get you by most card checkers. There are some gym rats with collections of cards, for spots they frequent all over the country. They simply whip out the appropriate one.

The Fire-Door Rap. Many gyms have auxiliary doors that are quite impassable from the outside but, thanks to fire marshals' decrees, can be easily opened from within. The key here is to knock on the door nearest some sympathetic player, who will obligingly admit you. With this method you're taking advantage of the fact that card checkers are usually stationed by locker-room doors, not gym doors.

The Familiarity Feint. Sometimes a casual nod to the card checker can get you by. Or, as you approach the gate, fix your eyes on someone—known or unknown—already within the inner sanctum and, like a regular, call out, "Hey, Walt, how ya doin'!" Better yet, find out the checker's name, saunter up to him or her, and deliver an effusive greeting, as if the two of you are old friends. The ensuing puzzled embarrassment is your chance to glide by.

The Chameleon. A broom, khakis, and keys are all you need for the look of a janitor, and a sport coat, tie, and 69¢ transistor radio earphone should make you over into a security guard. Wear your gym garb underneath.

The Left-Bank Method. A proven technique for sneaking into college gyms. Invest in a copy of Immanuel Kant's *The Critique of Pure Reason*—preferably a paperback edition, for that Bohemian touch—or some similarly scholarly tome. Dog-ear it heavily, and place it in your gym bag so that it conspicuously protrudes. Then find a buddy and, as soon as you're within sight of the checker, begin talking earnestly about some topic of academic import. Be sure your dialogue reaches an impassioned pitch just as you pass the checkpoint, and that you drop at least several of the following phrases within earshot: "epistemological," "Apollonian notion," "Manichean *Weltanschauung,*" and "determinism as opposed to free will." If you look too old to be a student, talk about your exegesis of vegetarianism in Tolstoy that will appear in the next number of *Daedalus,* and how you hope it will get you tenure. Only the most callous anti-intellectual would interrupt you for something so mundane as an ID check. And pleas of "I forgot my ID" are always a bit more believable after some highbrow phrase dropping.

The Cat Burglar's Entree. If you can find an open or unlocked window, consider getting through it your biggest obstacle. Once you do, you'll find that many gyms have accordion-style seats pushed right up against the wall, and it's two simple steps from windowsill to bleacher, and bleacher to bliss.

The Gender Jilt. If you're male and the checker is female, you can bolt by and lose yourself in the locker room before she can react. Works, of course, vice versa, too. The only problem with this method is you'll be a fugitive while you play, and may be *persona non grata* on subsequent visits.

The Gym-Lock Jam. The great moral lesson of the Watergate Affair: If you plan to break into something, don't tape the lock. It's too conspicuous. Try sticking some supple, not-too-terribly adhesive substance like bubble gum into the lock socket instead.

The Layered Look. If you wear your playing garb underneath street clothes and don't lug a gym bag around, you can use all sorts of pretenses to get in without arousing suspicion. Maybe you forgot something, or have to fetch someone; use your imagination to fashion a credible excuse. Once inside, simply shed a layer and call "winners."

The Backboard

The backboard is more than just a caddy to the game's metal-and-mesh receptacle, but far too often players consider rim height and the presence or absence of the net the only two variables that, from playground to playground, they should adapt to. If you bother to take the time to understand backboards, they can be very good to you.

The outdoor backboard is almost certainly going to be made of wood or wood composition, or metal, and shaped like a fan or rectangle. Metal boards, whether solid or perforated, offer a lively bounce, but you can never be absolutely sure of the surface; it's dented easily and dead spots can crop up anywhere. (If it seems as though regulars always know them, it may be because they're responsible for them: Ballplayers have been known to patiently use a hammer to create a personal deadspot.) Even a splintered or cracked wooden board is likely to provide a true return, though a warped one won't. The slipperier the surface, the livelier it's going to be, and the more backspin and arc should be added for sharp-angled bank shots. Remember, wood is generally not as slippery as metal. And backboard slappers and ball pinners are advised to temper their flamboyant style around weathered or splintered boards, for safety's sake.

LEFT:
The noble wooden backboard outlasts net, rim, and often players.

RIGHT:
Father Time gusjohnsoned this composition backboard.

Sometimes the high bank shot possible on its four-cornered counterpart is impossible on the fan board, and there's less of a linear guide for your eye on corner jumpers. But the "J" out of the deep corners, or from behind the backboard next to the baseline, needn't have quite so high a trajectory on the fan. (Still, the edges of a rectangular board, falling perpendicular to the asphalt, form the guidelines for corner jumpers that the fan doesn't supply.) Remember, too, that any backboard on a single pole easily becomes wobbly. Shoot banks off a wobbly board by aiming for a spot that's a little closer to you than your normal "sweet spot." The board will "give" a bit when your shot hits, but, as it swings back, it should give the ball that added push it needs to reach the hoop.

The board can also help you break out of a shooting slump. If your confidence is on the wane after several straight misses, use the backboard on your next few attempts. Good shooters, when they miss, usually miss long, and, by using the board, you'll make at least some contact with the scoring apparatus. When you find yourself deep under the board with the hoop barely in view, and it's tempting to think of the board as an extra defender, find an angle, use your imagination, and add a little spin. You'll soon discover and apply the Garbageman's Law: Backboard + Spin = Bucket.

Aging

Alas, after a certain age, every man is responsible for his face.
—Albert Camus

The process begins at birth, and the end result is the common denominator. In between lies all that garbage about the thrill of victory and the agony of defeat. Older players quickly become familiar with the agony of de feet. For them, pick-up ball is an affection of the heart, a way of keeping in shape, or both. It certainly isn't anything more glorious.

Around thirty, it's tempting to trade in your high-tops, gym shorts, and grubby T-shirts for the softer weekend world of perma-press tennis togs, double-knit golf attire, and Michelob. Many join the local softball circuit, where a midriff roll—a definite liability in hoops—becomes a respected symbol of power and status. Still others simply slide into armchairs and flick on the tube. But there are still some who keep chasing the game, like Allen Rothert, who chugs up and down a Richmond, Virginia, elementary school playground court with players half his age. Most of them watched him play from their classroom window as grade-schoolers years ago.

As the years catch up with you, you'll find that your D is first to go, around twenty-eight or twenty-nine. You'll catch yourself suggesting to younger teammates that your team play a zone. You'll perfect the reach-around, then the push, and soon you'll have mastered a completely new set of "fundamentals" to replace those nature is taking away.

Older players seem to fall into one of two categories. There are those who keep at it primarily for the exercise it provides. They find their way into the recreational leagues sponsored by Y's, church groups, and rec departments. They're often quite skilled, but the pace is half-speed, and fast breaks are all but outlawed, by common consent. Play produces zone defenses and the stand-still perimeter offenses that go hand in hand with zones. It's the closest the sport has come to spawning a "masters" competition for the geriatric, like those in golf, tennis, swimming, and track.

That other sort of elder is the one who keeps running with the kids. These old war-horses are a breed apart, and while most play with heaving chests, and sweat-soaked hair plastered to their foreheads, many are in excellent condition. And for what they lack in speed and agility they make up with savvy. They always seem to know how to get rebounding position, when to take the "J," how to catch their breath and save steps, and they all seem to have at least one sneaky play in their game. But they almost have to be able to take shortcuts. Middle age means your "availability" is literally a day-to-day proposition, at the whim of the weather. With cold, muscles tighten up, joints ache, ankles, knees, elbows, and wrists stiffen, and old injuries throb. Humid days cause similar annoyances. The best way to cope is—painfully enough—to stay home, check the weather reports, and wait for mild, dry weather.

You can prolong your playground career by playing exclusively half-court. Aside from the obvious—it's easier on the legs since it requires less running and accelerating—half-court gives the position player an edge. Experienced half-court players don't need the juices of youth to run clinics on basketball basics such as the give-and-go and back door. And standing "jump" shooters can showcase their specialty at one basket. As you get older, it takes a little longer to warm up, so it's essential to get on a winning team from the start. Losing can mean sitting, and sitting will mean muscles will tighten up again. It may be worthwhile to bag the crowded playground for a spot where the "comp" is a bit milder but you're assured of playing. It doesn't matter if you're unknown; you may

LEFT:
A makeshift rim, with a backboard that will provide little help.

RIGHT:
On a heavily used hoop like this one, a double rim would pay dividends.

be mistaken for a college coach prowling for scholarship candidates. Don't hesitate to play the role, since it could get you into a good—and long-lasting—run. You may find yourself getting compliments like "Nice pass, Coach" for executing the simplest of fundamentals. Just nod and smile.

The Rim

The rim is one thing to everyone at least once in his life: unreachable. During grade school, for all of us, it's too high to touch. For the rest of our lives, for most of us, it's too high to accommodate a jam. Lowering it would increase satisfaction everywhere, but devalue the dunk. And there's the abuse the goal would take from younger generations. Putting the ball through the rim is more than just one of the most pleasurable acts in the game; it's also a bench mark of sorts, something to touch, grab, or hang from. Players everywhere mark their growth by the moments they can touch the rim and jam the ball through it.

Many indulge in hanging from the rim because it's a macho sort of act, something that can intimidate. There's no better time to do it, either, than during that postcoital grace period: You can savor the delightful experience, and leave no doubt in anyone's mind as to who just slammed one through. But if you must act like a monkey, check over by the sandbox—there may be a jungle gym to satisfy that urge. Increasingly, double rims are being installed on playgrounds and, on heavily used courts where the action is constant and the rims get their share of abuse, pay dividends.

Those who treat an outdoor court as if it were a Romper Room should get the peer freeze, because damaged equipment poses problems for everyone. Bent rims, especially, just seem to hang there, like a fat lip pulled down to expose the pink interior. Lay-

Even a rusty tire rim can serve as a backyard goal.

ups and bank shots become trickier, since the front of the rim is now less inclined to redirect the ball back into the hoop. Instead, something played off the board is likely to roll right off the front of the rim and back into play. (The same regulars who hammer personal dead spots into metal backboards to accommodate bank shots may also give the front rim several hammer taps upward, creating a virtual conveyor belt to guide their bank shots from hand to hole.) Another annoying problem with the bent rim crops up during corner shots: With the rim tilted down toward the lane, the view from the corner is lopsided. This distracts the shooter's concentration, sometimes sufficiently to cause the shameful airball. You've got to imagine a cylinder yourself. Rims that are too high or low pose further problems. A high rim will cause a hitch for every shooter. A low rim, on the other hand, can be entertaining to play on, though it, too, may put the shooter's touch out of sync. Still, a low rim often makes a player feel taller, and living out this fantasy can be amply compensating in itself. Consider low rims, then, the lesser of two evils.

But also remember that debating the nuances of rims is a luxury. Players in rural areas have grown up on all kinds of substitutes: rusty tire rims tacked to tree trunks, or metal cylinders fashioned on slat boards and nailed to telephone poles or onto or inside barns. Rather than complaining about inconsistencies, the pick-up player should learn to adapt. Some rims will be too loose—the so-called sewer—and almost any shot will drop; others will be tight and accept only the softest of shots. About the only thing you can be sure of is that every official rim will allow two regulation-size balls, side by side, to pass through it. Remember *that* the next time you've missed five in a row.

Injuries

The best way to cope with injuries is to avoid getting them in the first place. If you play a kamikaze brand of ball, restrain yourself. When you make an aerial move through the lane, you're at the mercy of anyone with a mind to submarine you. Check out the supports and sidelines on unfamiliar courts before beginning to play. And don't think you can keep wearing socks with worn bottoms and still avoid the curse of blisters.

If you're in shape, you're less likely to get hurt. It's just that being in good physical condition isn't easy, since you really have to work at it. It means stretching, sit-ups, push-ups, running, and, for the very serious, working with weights. In any case, taking the time and putting in the effort should go a long way toward preventing muscle pulls, torn ligaments, and minor sprains. In the end, no one goes through a playground career unscathed. Learn about sports medicine. If you don't, you'll end up asking for advice you won't want to heed. Doctors, you see, will tell you to "stay off it" for a month when they don't understand that your getting back into action is as crucial to you as getting Jabbar back is to the Lakers.

Blisters. The shock of hard pounding and scraping at the beginning of the pick-up season can easily blister all but the most calloused areas of your feet. The juiciest blisters will appear on the ball of the foot, just below the big toe, and on the toe or back of the heel. Those who treat their own blisters have all butchered themselves at one time or another: First you take a needle, then sterilize it on a lit match, and finally puncture the blister to drain the fluid. But if you must work on your own blisters, pick up some zinc oxide from the pharmacy. When placed between the inner edge of the blister and the raw interior, it'll dry it up and speed healing. There are also "donuts"—disks of thick gauze with the center snipped out—that can be taped over the wounded area to prevent the blister from spreading its irritation (though donuts have a way of slipping loose after an hour of play). If you're lucky enough to have developed callouses, be sure to file them down regularly, so they don't develop blisters underneath.

Ankle Problems. Next to blisters, twisted ankles probably rate as the most common playground injury. Their causes: the uneven surfaces of many outdoor courts, and the debris scattered on them. You can usually tell the difference between a break and a sprain; the sprain, curiously enough, hurts more. The sensible approach to handling either injury calls for a visit to the doctor, who's sure to tell you, after wrapping the ankle in an Ace bandage and giving you crutches, to stay off it for a month. Don't get discouraged: Ballplayers have been known to return to action with a well-taped ankle in as little as four days.

Don't underestimate home remedies, either. Ice applied for several hours should keep most swelling under control. Another school of thought recommends taping the ankle immediately after the sprain occurs, on the theory that it will keep the swelling down even more. If you're constantly being plagued with ankle problems, keep plenty of tape and ice on hand. Taping your ankles before you play is a good preemptive move. If you've ever tried to tape your own ankle, you've probably found that, aside from the difficulty of doing figure-eights in reverse, your tape is always getting wrinkled and tangled. It's best to have someone help you. (Bandages are easier to work with than tape, but don't provide the same support.) If you want to avoid shaving your ankles before taping, simply pull on the top of a frazzled tube sock and tape right over it.

Jammed Fingers. The throbbing, swelling, and discoloration of this common ailment are always uncomfortable—and seem incurable—but home-style taping sometimes offers enough relief so that you can still handle the ball. Follow this rule, if you can: Only jam fingers on your weak hand.

Scrapes and Bruises. Bruised limbs and scraped knees and hands crop up all the time and simply must be endured. Try to avoid them by investigating the court's surface condition. Is there loose sand or gravel on it? Other slick spots where you could lose your footing and take a fall? When playing outdoors, diving for loose balls takes more nerve than desire. If you're a scrapper, you'll be a scraper, too, so keep some antiseptic and Band-Aids with your gear. Keep in mind that scrapes and bruises always seem to go away if you simply ignore them and play.

Knee Problems. They're much trickier than ankle problems, and it's best not to fool with them yourself. There are many kinds of knee braces available today, but—just this once—go see a doctor and let him prescribe one for you.

The Net

The net has a way of indicating the sociology of its surroundings. Well-kept suburban courts will feature nylon or cord nets, cradles for that staple of the suburbs, the backspin-laden jump shot. With the softer life comes a softer look and sound: The ball will nestle in the twine and produce that visually and aurally hypnotic "swish." The chain net, on the other hand, is as hardened as the urban life around it. Its very presence owes itself to park supervisors' expecting the worse in terms of use (constant) and abuse (from vandals, who'll readily snip and steal anything less sturdy than chain link). When the ball passes through, there's a harsh, metallic scratching sound or—on partially worn-away chain nets—almost a clank.

Too many hoops have no nets at all. To those unaccustomed to playing at a netless hoop, the rim will seem to be twelve feet high. It's an illusion that's enough to induce uncharacteristic drives out of suddenly tentative perimeter players. Some simply refuse to change their game and, rather than playing without that psycho-

LEFT:
A swish won't nestle in a plastic mesh net like this one.

RIGHT:
The rag of a worn out chain net can extract its own facial satisfaction, as one unsuspecting slam jammer discovered.

logically uplifting "swish" or "clank," bring their own nets to the park. But to do so is to admit to everyone on the court that you don't have that ability to adapt, and it'll cause your stock to plummet on the playground image exchange. So learn to hit the "J" on netless baskets. Regardless of how a hoop is dressed, you ought to be concentrating on the front of the rim; block everything else out of your mind. If it's that "silent swish" that irritates you, go for a bank shot, using the inside front of the rim to create the sound you seek.

And consider the unexpected advantages of netless rims. Nets, especially chain ones that cut and gouge fingers, can be hazardous to the skywalker's health. Part of a net hanging from a rim can be even more dangerous. Take the case of Ron Poacher. When you're sixteen, as Ron was, there's nothing quite as tempting as an 8½-foot hoop. Only this one, near San Antonio, had a little rag of a chain net left. When Poacher sailed in for some facial satisfaction, he got instead some unexpected dental extraction: Both of his upper eyeteeth caught on the net and were jerked cleanly out of his mouth. One came to earth some forty feet from the basket.

Cures

As yet, Jerry Lewis hasn't announced plans for a telethon, and the United Way has given no hint of support for research, but cures are needed for these playground ailments:

Hot Feet. No matter how many pairs of socks you wear, or how well ventilated your sneakers are, a few hours of playground ball on a sunny summer afternoon will really heat the feet up. Researchers please note: How about a solution that transfers heat from the feet to the hands?

Dry Mouth. If there's a drinking fountain nearby, more than often it's on the fritz.

Full Bladder. This especially becomes a problem when you have to sit out a few games.

But the antidotes to the following maladies have been discovered:

Sweaty Hands. Wipe them on the outside of your socks.

Car Keys. Run a shoelace through the hole on your key, or through the ring on your key chain, and simply let them jangle while you play.

Loose Change. If your hooping threads, like most ballplaying apparel, aren't equipped with deep pockets, a few coins will fit neatly between each pair of socks.

Light

Nature hasn't built any uniformity into the way she lights outdoor courts, so before getting involved in a game, check the location of the sun. Know where it's at its most bothersome, and force your man to that area, all the while avoiding that spot yourself. At midday, the sun shouldn't get in anyone's eyes, but the heat it gives off may well drain your body. As a result, twilight is one of the most pleasant times of day to play ball. The strength of the sun's rays has diminished, and a light breeze is often in the air. But the sun can be at its trickiest, especially if it's setting behind one of the backboards. If you see two squads running full court, odds are the one with the sun at its back—all other things being equal—is going to emerge the winner. If you find yourself in a twilight run, do what football captains do when they win the coin flip on a gusty day: Barter away first possession to get the favor of the elements.

As twilight turns to dusk, and dusk to darkness, routine chest passes get lost in midflight and then seem to come suddenly upon you. Though many parks have artificial lighting, its quality will be as varied and mercurial as the crowd in the corner playing craps. When running under the lights, be as sensitive as you would be when confronted with the sun: Learn the angles of the lights' beams, know where the dark corners are, and adjust your game accordingly.

Where there's a will there's a way, and when no lights exist—or when a parsimonious city refuses to turn them on—the hardcore have been known to produce their own remedies. Many hoops become transplanted to telephone poles closer to streetlights. And some players park their cars next to the court and run the headlights off the battery.

The sun can be fickle in the way it lights courts, changing with the time of day and season of the year. (Robert F. Rodriguez, Gannett Westchester Newspapers)

Warming Up

Warming up does more than just get the kinks out of your limbs and help you find the range on your "J." If you want to play in the

next game, warm-up time is show-off time; if you know you'll be playing soon, it's take-stock time—especially if you've got "winners" and have a few spots to fill. It can be very chaotic. If everyone at the park has brought his own ball, you know what you'll suffer through: a bong on the head when you venture underneath to retrieve yours; a twenty-footer with perfect backspin all set to drop that gets displaced by another imperialistic shot an instant before it enters the cylinder; those rare, almost mystical moments when two shots fall through simultaneously and hang, in bulbous suspension, in the net until someone with a third ball jars them free.

But for all its apparent disorganization, even warm-ups have their own rules. On suburban and small-town courts, especially, anyone sinking anything more challenging than a lay-up is likely to have the ball returned to him for another, as a "courtesy." And other playgrounds warm up according to "rules of the court"— meaning you shoot until you miss, take a lay-up, and then rebound for someone else. The more players there are, the less likely it is

Dark corners and sudden passes are two problems that can crop up on artificially lit courts.

Warming up means getting the kinks out and finding the range.

OPPOSITE PAGE:
Bulky clothing and raw fingers are two inconveniences the off-season player has to deal with.

that these conventions will be honored. When there's a crowd at one hoop and only one ball among it, playing a mass game of Twenty-one or Free-for-All is a good way to warm up.

While loosening up, if you know you'll be playing in the next game, do a bit of reconnaissance. What's the backboard like? Loose? Resilient? And the rim—is it bent or loose? Check for sunspots on the court, so you can avoid them once the game begins, and steer your opponent that way. Also be sure to note those treacherous patches of dirt or gravel that might sabotage a spin move. And take your warm-ups with a ball that's likely to be used once a game starts. Some lopsided balloon won't be used if there's something better around, so don't warm up with it.

Weather

We're not going to question why you'd want to play on a court right after it's rained rather than waiting for it to dry. We understand. Use puddles as picks, and run your man into them. The danger of a slip and consequent ankle turn is counterbalanced by the better grip you'll get on the ball. If you feel safer drying the court before playing on it, try a broom to spread out puddles and speed up evaporation (though a squeegee is more effective), and do away with that moist film by mopping it up with old towels. If this proves insufficient—or if you simply don't have the patience—pour kerosene over the wet area and put a match to it.

Wintertime ballplaying is all but hopeless in the intemperate North. Even when there's no snow on the ground, you'll find it hard to simply cock for a shot in a down-filled coat. And if your favorite schoolyard is also used for parking or recess, snowplows will set back the *real* coming of spring by several weeks, by pushing snow up against the basket supports. When balmy weather comes, these snow heaps—right under the hoops—are the last to melt. During the fall and spring you'll have to deal with high winds. Try limiting yourself to lay-ups, bank shots, and the low-arched "J" with plenty of backspin.

8. SCHOOLYARD CHIC

Fashion

Basketball in its element is a game of sartorial spartanism: Jocks, socks, shorts, and sneaks have always sufficed. But that hasn't kept players from embellishing the game's simple sportswear, much of which can be gussied up. It starts with the simplest canvas basketball shoes. The high-topped white shoe wears pastel-colored shoelaces particularly well. The darker canvas hues—blue, purple, and black—acquire their own flourishes in time: the telltale white crust formed by ebbing, evaporated perspiration. Adolescent hands scrawl nicknames and uniform numbers of idols in indelible marker. A pair of sneakers may look like a grafitti-free rest-room wall upon purchase, but soon they will become cluttered with "Iceman" and "Dr. J" instead of vulgar epigrams, and "44" and "6" instead of phone numbers to call for a good time.

Scribblings like these would never be appropriate on leather shoes, which generally appear outdoors either in the twilight of a predominantly indoor career ("Got to wear 'em out before I get a new pair") or on the feet of the wealthy. Instead of the salty residue, their mark of service is a series of cracks in the material, where the shoe was forced to bend but the leather offered no suppleness. Once a leather pair is broken in, canvas shoes can't come close to matching their comfort.

But there's something reassuringly American about canvas shoes. Take the Converse All Star, for instance. Until Converse introduced a trendy chevron-and-star design, there was always red-and-blue-striped siding on each sole, and heraldry—the blue star and "Chuck Taylor" in immaculate cursive—just behind the niche for the anklebone. The two eyelets on the side of each shoe looked like portholes on a yacht, and the "Made in U.S.A." imprint on the heel served as a certification, leaving no doubt about this asphalt-going vessel's port of origin. While many are seduced by Nike, Puma, Adidas, and other exotic-sounding brand names, a solid corps remains true, if only because "Converse" is a practical word, present in Webster's as both a noun and a verb, and it doesn't sound like some Visigothic horde's battle cry.

Certain cuts and colors of canvas shoes indicate playing styles, and a quick glance at a pair of feet almost serves as a thorough

Everything but tie-dyed jockstraps

scouting report. Low-topped whites are, like sports cars, sleek and streamlined. They identify a player who tends to channel his playing energies in a horizontal manner. Beware of excellent moves to the basket and the unleashing of sudden, pinpoint passes.

You can assume anyone in black is not the flashy type. Aggressive, defensive-minded guards wear low black Oxfords. A look at the heel will reveal its Achilles side: "Overplay me to the left, be-

There are stylish ways of covering more than just your feet.

cause I'm right-handed and can't dribble with my left hand," the shoes seem to say. Black high-tops, the laces cross-hatching their way up the foot and asphyxiating the ankle like Johnny Unitas' football shoes, are the mark of an immobile frontcourtman. (Not until "Tiny" Archibald began wearing high blacks in the early 1970s did this style seem appropriate for basketball's little men; it seemed that much of Archibald's appeal had been the nimbleness he demonstrated in spite of what seemed to be the disadvantage of playing basketball in football shoes.) High-topped white shoes conjure up the most favorable images: a pure jump shot, excellent change of direction, and fine leaping ability. Concerns that they were too elemental—something Mom may have picked up at a Korvette White Sale—were quickly dispelled when pictures of Bill Bradley wearing a pair seeped onto the NBA scene. If they were good enough for a Rhodes scholar and banker's son, they were good enough for you.

Wearers of high-tops are experienced, wise, or both. If they started in low cuts, they've likely been hurt and become converts. Those who persist in wearing lows either haven't yet had their first bad ankle sprain or are trying to commit suicide. And if your opponent hasn't even bothered to tie his shoes or—worse yet—is

wearing them with a crushed heel, he takes you for a lightweight.

There are stylish ways of covering more than just your feet. The first rule to learn about lettered pick-up wear—and T-shirts in particular—is "Don't say where you play." In other words, if the T-shirt you're thinking of wearing to the park has some personal significance, or has the name of a team you've played for emblazoned on it, leave it in its drawer. (And vice versa: That's why you see so many hackers with chic UCLA BASKETBALL wear.) This is a convention of mysterious origin; whether it first sprang up to camouflage talent, or was simply a rite of modesty, no one knows. In any case, it's as immutable a maxim for the fashion conscious as that which rules against mixing checks and plaids.

Shirts from rec leagues in which you've participated are exempt from this proviso, for some reason, while T-shirts from all-star games in which you've *never* played, or jerseys graced with flippant, basketball-related slogans you want to put on and get off your chest, make up the *haute couture* of the schoolyard. Shirts boosting sneaker manufacturers, on the other hand, once popular attire, are now considered slightly tacky, and those that allude to lesser sports are *toga non grata*, particularly on city playgrounds. Also, be sure that anything sleeveless you wear is a basketball top,

not a tank top. Tank-top straps are spaced farther apart than basketball jersey straps and tend to fall effeminately off shoulders.

Below the waist, simple gym shorts remain the most popular way of complying with laws against indecent exposure. Insignia on trunks are generally less conspicuous than that on T-shirts, so the "Don't say where you play" rule can be relaxed accordingly. You can tell a lot about how someone plays by what sort of pants he wears. Unless the weather is frigid and everyone's wearing them, long sweat pants suggest a seriousness of purpose—the wearer is out to lose some weight or get a good workout, or both. Sweats cut off evenly at or just above the knee forbode a graceless but effective style, while jaggedly cut sweats indicate a preference for run-and-gun. A good rule of thumb for judging clowns wearing cut-off football pants: The shorter they've been cut off, the tougher he thinks he is. Long janitorial pants in either khaki or blue-green— with white sneaks absolutely *de rigueur* on the feet—are becoming increasingly popular among gym rats, and for outdoor play during the fall and spring. Gym shorts over long sweats is another popular combination for cool-weather wear. And rolling one—*just* one— pant leg up is a fad that persists on inner-city playgrounds, where so much ballplaying is done in long pants.

After a span of years during which tube socks seemed to crawl higher up calves and take on gaudier pigmentation with each passing season, the sock scene has come full circle: Less is more, and classic white—pulled no higher than the base of the calf—is very much "in" again. Not that there can't be any color in hooping hose; it's just that these days, six, seven, or eight bands of pastels between ankle and knee is about as apropos as paisley. Instead many hoopers are striving for a hybridized look that has a pair of reasonably sober tube socks on the inside and plain white wool outside. And don't underestimate the contribution of shoelaces to your appearance. One of Luther "Ticky" Burden's ticks was wearing tassles on his Cons. Style is as important as color; by all means, don't be straight-laced.

Of all the fashionable accountrements that crop up on street players, there is none less functional than the sweatbands that circumscribe wrists and brows. The wristband, in particular, has no reason other than cosmetic for appearing on players' wrists, despite all the arguments apologists advance on behalf of its ability to keep your shooting hand dry. The headband is only slightly less ornamental, though it does help to tame unruly locks. Tennis hats with turned-down brims and—during cool weather—knit wool

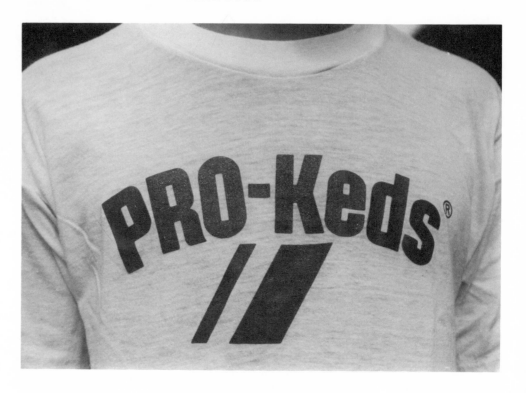

caps handsomely top off any basketball ensemble, though they're not much more practical than sweatbands. Visored caps are out, though, since their bills interfere with the first movement of the arms upward for the "J," unless you wear them backward, in the Johnny Bench mode. (If you do, be sure to turn the visor *up*.)

Music

As he was growing up in Detroit, there was one song that told NBA guard Jimmy McElroy that, in his words, "it was time to play ball." It was Marvin Gaye's "I Heard It Through the Grapevine." (In fact, Marvin Gaye himself was an occasional participant in pick-up games at the Ceciliaville Rec Center in the Motor City.) For many others, there's also a special tune with a beat that they associate with an exceptional game, or the summer months of some vintage year when the pick-up ball was especially good. Both basketball and music are founded on rhythmic schemes; basketball, particularly the run-and-gun brand of the streets, is often cited as choreography for jazz, one of the freest musical forms. The thump of the dribble is the ground bass, and a 360-degree dipsy-do in the lane is an improvisatorial riff.

Style is important: By all means don't be straight-laced.

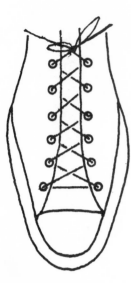

Straight. *For what it lacks in flair it makes up in support of the ankle.*

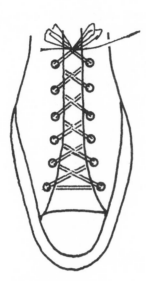

Soul. *Straight times two— red and green laces on black canvas shoes is the preferred color arrangement.*

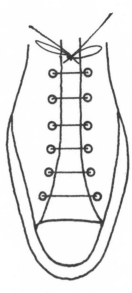

Window. *A clean look, particularly popular among wearers of low canvas shoes.*

Super Soul. *Window tim two—again, wear the proper color scheme for the best effect.*

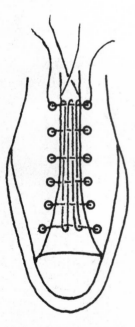

New York Basket Weave. *One lace is strung in the window style, and another is woven in and out, up and down—then pull tight and tie all the loose ends.*

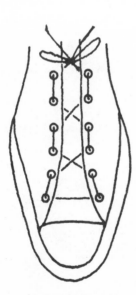

Vertical. *All the cross- hatching is done under- neath the upper, so it's a bit uncomfortable and there's not much support.*

Sister Half Hitch. *A lad- der-like stitch, with ele- ments of the window and vertical looks.*

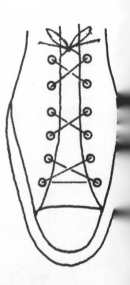

Double—or Triple— Cross. *You need an o number of eyelet row this to come out corre*

But pop music is the food of face, and it plays on. Whether it's the unabashed funk of the Ohio Players ("When you're hot, you're hot, you really shoot your shot"), the inspiring strains of Chuck Brown and the Soul Searchers ("When the Fat Lady sings, we'll do it in game number seven"), or the facile appropriateness of Jay and the Techniques' "Keep the Ball Rollin'," the ubiquitous "box" is likely to crank out something to fit the on-court action. The "box" isn't always a portable system that gets propped up against a fence. Suburban kids have mobile boxes; they magnetize car speakers, afix them to their car doors, and run the stereo off the battery. But live music always beats the "box." McElroy and fellow Detroiters Spencer Haywood, George Gervin, and Campy Russell learned the game at the rec center by the Brewster Projects, on whose corners fabled acts like the Supremes and the Four Tops came up.

Visored caps are only chic when they're worn backward in the Johnny Bench mode.

The Country Look:
Cowlick (optional); horn-
rimmed glasses; facial hair
(preferred); regional fran-
chise T-shirt (plaid flannel
warm-up optional); cut-
offs (snipped just above
the knee); one pair of
socks, rumpled, uneven,
and half pulled up; beat-
up Cons.

No box is necessary for on-court *a cappella,* which is a great way to rattle an opponent. If your man triple pumps a creative shot that nonetheless embarrassingly misses the mark, head downcourt softly crooning several bars of the Temptations' "Just My Imagination," with the pronouns appropriately altered, of course: "It was just your 'magination, runnin' away with you."

If you're trailing by a couple of hoops in a game of One-on-One, a few variations on Rare Earth's theme, "Your Love is Fading," can have quite a cumulative psychological effect. Hit a "J" and sing: "Your lead is fading." Hit another and add: "Baby, I can feel your lead fade." Then take your man inside for the refrain: "It goes right in your face, now you just can't hold your place—oooh, Lord, you're losing it."

And Carly Simon's "Anticipation," with the syllables all strung out, may be just the word to embellish a cat-quick steal at midcourt, and the breakaway lay-up that follows it.

The Inner-City Look: Knit wool cap; ABA ball; sweatband on wrist; medallion around neck; neighborhood T-shirt; jaggedly-cut-off sweatpants; solid white socks, pulled high; serious sneaks.

The Female Look:
Hair pulled back in pony-
tail; older brother's T-
shirt, untucked; hand-me-
down gym shorts; latest in
hose; high basketball
shoes.

*The Wrong Look:
A perm (the white man's
"'fro"); dark-rimmed
glasses with no safety
strap; long sleeve button-
down shirt, with the top
buttoned and the tails
tucked in; tube of first aid
cream; a watch with a
sweep second hand (for
making three-second
calls); gym shorts with the
piping tucked up; black
nylon socks; jogging shoes.*

9. DOERS' PROFILES

*Twelve who brought
palms together*

EVERY city has a ballplayer whose exploits are legend in the streets but not beyond them. Peers lionize him, while wiser neighborhood elders—who have witnessed the short, mercurial careers of other urban superstars—mutter things beginning with "if he had only" every time his name comes up. In the end, misdirected ambition, drugs, a "raw deal," another career, or just plain fate derails him, and his only solace comes from followers who keep maintaining that their "man" could take it to this pro or that pro any day.

In many little-known cases, they probably could. And sometimes they did: Hoop connoisseurs savor those moments when a local player wins a permanent spot in every spectator's mind by pulling a facial on some visiting pro. With no "face" to gain and a whole lot to lose, and with the damage an unexpected slide on the asphalt can do to $200,000-per-annum legs, fewer and fewer pros are letting overnight reputations develop at their expense. But a face job against the best will grant the administrator immediate status, with the details of the move exaggerated a bit more in every retelling until it becomes an established part of urban folklore.

What follows are profiles of city players who made a name for themselves by answering spectators' calls to "do it." It's not really an all-time, all-playground team, but rather a sampling of players from around the country whose ability never got the exposure it deserved. We don't know what brand of scotch they drank, but we do know they brought palms together.

Joe Hammond

NICKNAME: "The Destroyer"
CITY: New York
VINTAGE: late 60s–70s
DESCRIPTION: A lithe, coffee-colored guard who stands about 6'1". The Destroyer always manages to keep the big men happy by dishing off, so they return the favor by giving him first dibs on outlet passes. Drives as well as he shoots.
CAREER: No college experience, but holds the Rucker League single-game record of 71 points, set in 1977. Turned down a contract from the Lakers, reportedly because it lacked a no-cut clause.
MEMORABLE FACIAL: In a summer league game at the Rucker battleground, Hammond tap-dunked home a teammate's miss after sailing laterally through the lane, while pros like Doctor J stood idly by.

Herman Knowings

NICKNAME: "Helicopter"
CITY: New York
VINTAGE: 60s–mid-70s
DESCRIPTION: A 6'4" front-court skywalker who patrolled lanes and baselines all over Harlem, Knowings performed most spectacularly on D, rejecting shots. Tree-trunk-like calves and thighs enabled him to do his levitation thing.
CAREER: Exclusively playground. Explains one Harlemite: "College ain't for everybody."
MEMORABLE FACIAL: In a Rucker League game, Helicopter went for a ball fake in the lane. As his man waited for him to come down, Herman treaded air, witnesses swear, until the referee whistled a three-second violation.

Floyd Brady

NICKNAME: "All Night"
CITY: unpredictable—prowls the Northeast
VINTAGE: 60s–70s
DESCRIPTION: A barrel-chested, bespectacled power forward. Just 6'2" and, due to near-sightedness, a poor outside shooter, but amazingly effective in close quarters. Often plays while wearing a tennis hat.
CAREER: A noteworthy few years at little Hope College prompted some interest from the old Hawks of St. Louis. Says Brady: "My attorney advised me to hold out for a no-cut contract. I'm still holding out." In the meantime, All Night has been to divinity school, and is now a rev.
MEMORABLE FACIAL: Caught under the hoop, Brady went through a series of head fakes and body pumps before making a half-turn and skying. Even though a defender clotheslined him—laying him parallel to the ground in midair—Brady not only got the shot off but saw it drop through *and* managed to utter his characteristic "All night!" while falling into a heap on the floor.

Tracy Gunning

NICKNAME: "Gunner"
CITY: Jersey Shore
VINTAGE: 70s
DESCRIPTION: A 5'5" stocky, freckle-faced guard who wears five pairs of socks and was asked to play for her high school's men's team. Quick hands on D, and triple pumps on O.
CAREER: Scored 1,000 points at St. Catherine's Grammar School and then led St. Rose High to two New Jersey state championships. Seton Hall won out in the bidding war.
MEMORABLE FACIAL: In a Jersey showdown with 6'8" Anne Donovan, Gunner poured in 32 points, many on off-balance, twisting up-and-under drives right at and around her towering nemesis.

Steven Strother

NICKNAME: "Stro"
CITY: Boston
VINTAGE: 70s
DESCRIPTION: A strong guard, just over six feet, with a knack for slipping inside, muscling up a lay-up, and drawing the three-point play. A devastating outside shooter, too—when he's hot. As one coach says: "Stro can shoot you out of a game as fast as he can shoot you into one."
CAREER: Strother's penchant for one-on-one had him collecting splinters on the Providence bench. Still, Houston drafted him and, even though he's in his late twenties, he's been preparing himself for one last shot at the bigs by honing his skills in several summer leagues.
MEMORABLE FACIAL: In one pick-up game, Stro drove the lane and, as he jumped and leaned in to take a right-handed eight-footer, a big man loomed in his way. In midair, Strother switched the ball to his left hand and—on his way down—threw in an underhanded scoop shot.

Marvin Washington

NICKNAME: "Stickman"
CITY: Lexington
VINTAGE: early 60s–70s
DESCRIPTION: Truly deserving of his nickname, Washington is a 5'9" 120-pound pure point guard with a great handle. He dishes well, shoots like a trooper, and plays the Karate Defense, which he invented.
CAREER: Four normal years of play in high school along with—this isn't so normal—twenty-five straight in Lexington summer leagues. Now almost forty and in better shape than most people half his age, Stickman holds almost all Dirt Bowl career records.
MEMORABLE FACIAL: Stickman administers facials that are feats of endurance as well as works of art: He has been known to go one-on-one for twenty-four straight hours without eating or sleeping.

Art Hicks

NICKNAME: "Big Art"
CITY: Chicago
VINTAGE: 50s–mid-70s
DESCRIPTION: A spirited monster of a man (6'5", 250 pounds) who plays every position on the court well.
CAREER: A high school All-American at the now-defunct St. Elizabeth High School in Chi-town, Hicks bounced from Northwestern to Seton Hall before finding a niche in the gyms along Lake Michigan.
MEMORABLE FACIAL: With a single one-on-two break at the Windy City's Martin Luther King Boys' Club, Big Art was responsible for a gymful of shattered glass and awed spectators. He'd taken off from the foul line with the ball and gusjohnsoned it.

Earl Manigault

NICKNAME: "Goat"
CITY: New York
VINTAGE: mid-60s–mid-70s
DESCRIPTION: A 6'2" jumping-jack forward who artistically blended the gyroscopic floor movements of Earl the Pearl with the aeronautic creativity of Doctor J. More jams in him than a case of Mason jars after your grandmother got through with them.
CAREER: A season on the bench at Johnson C. Smith University and an abortive tryout with the Utah Stars of the old ABA sandwiched around a heroin-induced prison stay. He made a courageous effort to keep others from meeting his own fate by organizing a short-lived summer tournament that bore his nickname.
MEMORABLE FACIAL: In the mid-60s, just as he was beginning to develop a rep, Goat went up against a squad of his seniors in a tourney game. Off a break, he approached the rim from straight on, and two-hand slam-jammed the ball over two guys who stood 6'6" and 6'8". The crowd held up the game for five minutes with its reaction.

Leslie Scott

NICKNAME: "Great"
CITY: Baton Rouge
VINTAGE: 60s–early 70s
DESCRIPTION: A slim, 6'3" swingman who would psychologically devastate opponents before physically devastating them: Followers claim he never missed a shot while warming up. Once a game began, he'd do it with a low, line-drive "J" and a hook that was automatic out to half court.
CAREER: After pouring in twenty-nine a game for the Loyola of Chicago frosh, Great Scott quit school and retreated to the Louisiana playgrounds. Turned down an offer from the Globetrotters and now works on an offshore oil rig.
MEMORABLE FACIAL: In a tight half-court game, Scott had the ball deep in the corner with his back to the basket. With two defenders all over him, he leaped, spun, and threw in a line drive to win the game.

Skyles Runser

NICKNAME: "Sky High"
CITY: San Francisco
VINTAGE: 70s
DESCRIPTION: Puts on spectacular shows in midair, most notably with his feared Blind Wraparound Pass. While opponents take shelter in anticipation of his feared tomahawk, Sky High, a mere six-footer, will deceive and make-believe before dishing out his magical assists.
CAREER: Highly recruited out of high school, Runser chose to remain on the playgrounds, "where the real ball is played." Still feeding his basketball jones.
MEMORABLE FACIAL: As time was running out in a Bay Area summer league game, Runser was double-teamed in the corner with no escape humanly possible. So he tried the inhuman, going "sky high," making a 180-degree turn, and lofting a perfect lob pass for the game-winning slam jam.

Lewis Lloyd

NICKNAME: "Black Magic"

CITY: Philadelphia

VINTAGE: 70s

DESCRIPTION: A small forward who prefers stuffs 'n' snuffs to ground maneuvers. Score-keepers at Sonny Hill League games used this formula for predicting his stats: His point total will equal his rebound total. Since each will be over twenty, you can usually get his blocked shot total by dividing that number by three.

CAREER: The Hill League and a southwestern military school have rehabilitated him after a rocky academic career in high school. At last reports he was at Drake, filling them up.

MEMORABLE FACIAL: In a high school all-star game in Ohio some years back, Black Magic got the ball in the foul circle, flashed his characteristic smile ("Nothin' cocky," his disciples insist, "just a sign that he knows what he's gonna do"), and took it to and over 6'10" DeWayne Scales. The take nearly broke Lloyd's wrist.

Arthur Johnson

NICKNAME: "Chuckie"

CITY: Cincinnati

VINTAGE: 70s

DESCRIPTION: At 6'5" and 190 pounds, Chuckie dominates centers much taller than he. When word of his jumping ability got around, as many Air Force recruiters as college scouts were after him, according to rumors in the streets.

CAREER: Had an impressive high school record but, as a mischievous college student, Chuckie drifted from one school to another before finally finishing up at Oklahoma Christian. Now does his drifting back in Cincy, from playground to gym to playground, playing pick-up.

MEMORABLE FACIAL: During one game, Johnson administered one on himself. He went up so high for a rebound that he slashed the underside of his armpit on the rim on his way down. A doctor of the medical sort needed eight stitches to close the wound.

10. STALKING BIG GAMES

Give me them that will face me.
—Falstaff, in Shakespeare's Henry IV, Part I

Where the good runs are, from coast to coast

If you're looking for a game, as Falstaff may have been doing, worry about the comp later. Your first task is to find a court. That in itself may be a challenge; people in power decide how to spend public funds for recreation, and people in power don't play basketball. (In the suburbs, especially, you'll pass umpteen tennis courts before catching a glimpse of the reassuring half-moon.) Your best bets are towns that have good basketball traditions. They're more likely to have fine outdoor spots, and indoor facilities that stay open, than football or tennis towns. Most big cities have large public parks adorned with basketball slabs, municipally run rec centers, or at least a YMCA, and it's safe to say there's hardly a college in the country without a gym. So if you're an itinerant type who's just got the itch to play ball, you should be able to run down a hoop without going cold turkey.

Taos, New Mexico

Manhattan's Upper East Side

   Good comp is another matter. Caliber and style vary depending on where you play—city or suburb, indoor or outdoor—and even when you play. Indoor action runs year round, with some of the best comp cropping up in college gyms. The ideal time is out of basketball season but while school is still in session. During the fall, varsity team members and would-be members are playing feverishly to get into shape, and they're expectant with a season to come. Springtime games on campuses are more casual, and often filled with imitators of the protagonists of the college and professional championships that are playing themselves out on TV at the same time. Big-city Y's and municipal gymnasiums provide comp of comparable caliber, though the players may not be as serious or team-oriented as the well-schooled collegians. Though some YMCA crowds tend to be a bit on the old side, people have known good games can be found there since long before that hit song.

Carneysville, Georgia

And neighborhood community centers and Boys' Clubs offer a younger crowd—high- and junior-high-schoolers, and a few recent grads with a rep to uphold—but may demand more patience on your part if you're a stickler for fundamental ball.

College gyms and Y's usually boast habitual noontime crowds, guys with incipient ulcers from having wolfed down their lunches so they can make it to the gym in time to get in a game. This brand of pick-up play develops a strict code of conduct, intense day-to-day rivalries, and a surprisingly high level of team play—largely because of everyone's familiarity with one another. As soon as 1 P.M. rolls around, the proceedings come to an abrupt halt, and no one lingers—not out of any unwillingness to play longer, but from the certainty that the same action will be available the next day. Lunch-hour hoop is a workday groove that neutralizes the workday grind. On weekends, suburban commuters often fare best by corralling a kid in the neighborhood and asking if there's some action in his driveway. For the unfamiliar, driveway ball means puddles, a corner filled with crab apples, and a tree branch that always manages to deflect the J. For your youthful host, it likely means getting Dad to install a carport light, and making sure it has a base that swivels and can be pointed upward, toward the hoop, for nighttime play. And it means "free-ins" and a trump of a H-O-R-S-E shot taken from back of the garbage cans.

Back on the playgrounds, the outdoor scene is sometimes hard to gauge. In San Francisco, for instance, there's one place to play—Funston Playground—and everyone knows it; in New York City, on the other hand, there are prime spots in several boroughs, and the hoopster looking for the best game will have to keep an ear to the street to find out "where they be runnin' at today." If one spot acquires a first-rate reputation, parks departments will often do their best to maintain the court surface and replace worn nets. As a result, that park will solidify its rep (a good example: Shawnee Park in Louisville). Neighborhoods-in-transition create a melting pot of playing styles that raises the quality and richness of play across the board (check out Foster Park in Brooklyn). And ballplayers from one part of a city aren't intimidated from journeying to an outdoor facility in an unfamiliar neighborhood if it's good enough (e.g., Meadowood Park in suburban Speedway, near Indianapolis).

Apply a little amateur demography and sociology if you're suddenly in a strange city and want to find a game to suit you. You can be sure a park in a ghetto will feature a fast-paced style of ball; a

Shelby County, Indiana

suburban spot is likely to have a jumper-oriented, work-the-ball-for-a-good-shot sort of game. If either style suits you, you know where to go first. Courts sandwiched between city and suburb are known to offer an appealing mixture of types, all out for nothing but the elusive "good run." Because it's a mixed group, it's also less likely to engender the kind of clannishness that many neighborhood-oriented parks foster, and which tends to make the drop-in player or new kid in town feel like more of an outsider than he already is.

Outdoors, the season is shorter, the scrapes more painful, and the variables, well, more variable. But on a summer evening, with the sun setting over the baseline, there's no player with any feeling for the game who would prefer a stuffy gym. What follows is a geographic sampling—*just* a sampling—of America's finest basketball playgrounds, with information about competition, conven-

A summer evening, with the sun setting over the baseline. (Rick Potter)

tions, and facilities available at each. For places where the bulk of the ballplaying is done indoors, that fact has been noted along with the top spots. The symbols are keyed this way:

WHERE IT'S AT
Urban 

Suburban, Shorefront, or Campus

Small town or Rural

BEST COMP
Occasional pro or Top-flight college 

Average college or Top-flight high school

Average high school or Recreational adult

Junior high or Hacker

HOOPS AND SLABS
6/8   Number of baskets/Number of full courts

RACK AND TWINE
Level rim with net

Level rim without net

Bent rim with net

Bent rim without net

GOTTA WIN BY TWO
Games played according to "Deuce"

MAKE IT TAKE IT
Games played according to "Winners' Out"

LIGHT AT NIGHT
Court equipped with working lights

REFRESHMENTS
Working drinking fountain nearby

GIRLS
Women play often

LOOP
Organized summer league

Yankee

Up New England way, don't put too much stock in that stereotype about the rugged individualist—at least not on the basketball court. Oh, they're rugged, all right, but they don't go in much for One-on-One. And except in cities like Boston—where the pick-up players have been hardened by turning back invasions of imperialistic street hockey players—teams holding court for two games will often gallantly defer to a waiting team rather than insisting on a third run. Long winters shorten the outdoor hooping season, and slabs are frequently desecrated by hoses that turn them into hockey rinks.

Darby Park
Washington and Willard
Boston, Massachusetts

 6/3

The neighborhood is as tough to crack as the game. The hub of Dorchester's drug traffic is up the street a block, where a different sort of shooting up and getting high is done.

Washington Park
Martin Luther King and Washington
Boston, Massachusetts

 8/4

Once the premier spot in Beantown, Wash Park is now a BYON facility—Bring Your Own Net—with a new, oft-used gym next door.

South Park
Locust
Burlington, Vermont

  4/2

Even if you hit these courts on an off day, you'll probably find Doug Atkins, a self-styled recreation director, there shooting a few.

Corporal Burns Playground
Flagg and Memorial
Cambridge, Massachusetts

  4/2

A typical team here will feature a local Bogarter, a set-shooting Harvard scholar of Afghanian Nationalism, and a quick-handed mechanic (quantum, that is—Ph.D. MIT). The city does not provide refreshments.

Washington Park
Mitchell and Meridian
Groton, Connecticut

  4/2

The action here is best on weekday evenings during the summer. Full court Five-on-Five is the most popular game, played to fifteen by ones.

Falmouth Heights Court
On-the-Beach
Falmouth Heights, Massachusetts

2/1

Hoopage, Cape Cod style, with the beach just across the street. The rims run like the tide: One is high, the other low.

Ash Street School
Maple and Ridge
Manchester, New Hampshire

  2/1

There are better facilities in town, but this is where the better players run.

WHERE IT'S AT

 Urban

 Suburban, Shorefront or Campus

 Small town or Rural

BEST COMP

 Occasional pro or Top-flight college

 Average college or Top-flight high school

 Average high school or Recreational Adult

 Junior high or Hacker

HOOPS AND SLABS

6/8 Number of baskets/Number of full courts

RACK AND TWINE

 Level rim with net

 Level rim without net

 Bent rim with net

 Bent rim without net

MISCELLANEOUS

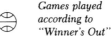 Games played according to "Deuce"

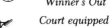 Games played according to "Winner's Out"

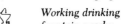 Court equipped with working lights

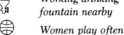 Working drinking fountain nearby

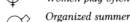 Women play often

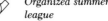 Organized summer league

Woodstock Recreation Center, Woodstock, Vermont

Doering Oaks Park
Park
Portland, Maine

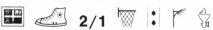 2/1

Located in the city's largest park complex, in the center of Portland. You can stumble into a decent game here on weekday evenings.

Evans Field
Smith
Providence, Rhode Island

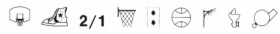 2/1

Ernie D, Marvin B, and a host of Providence College hotshots, present and former, are among the ranks. Don't worry, there aren't any old tire irons lying around.

Wolcott Park
New Britain
West Hartford, Connecticut

  4/2

A very nice facility where former Celtic Steve Bulkin learned his trade.

Woodstock Recreation Center
Route 4
Woodstock, Vermont

 2/1

The finest outdoor spot in northern New England, and the comp is better than you'd expect in a town of 3,000. But be careful: The nearby Ottauquechee will carry errant cross-court passes downriver to the end of the world, Taftsville.

Cousy Court
Crompton Park
Worcester, Massachusetts

 2/1

Shots here go up with gobs of backspin—because of the "soft" rims—and passes are delivered from behind the back, as homage to the court's namesake.

Mid-Atlantic

Action along this strip starts on the Jersey Shore at The Headliner Bar in Neptune (where the court is catered, and "taste that" may be a bittersweet double entendre) and stretches down to Virginia Beach. There's a whole lot in between: Philly—Sonny Hill Country—and its Sherwood Rec Center; Baltimore, where the Fat Lady sings indoors every night at the Madison Square Rec Center (games to fifty, by twos); along with D.C. and environs. Keep in mind that many in this region—especially Marylanders and Virginians—prefer "straight" to "deuce."

Maplewood–Alta Vista Rec Center
Alta Vista and Wisconsin
Bethesda, Maryland

 8/4

The summer league here has a good local "rep," and pick-up games are played to a time limit, not a set score.

Narberth Rec Board Court
Haverford and Conway
Narberth, Pennsylvania

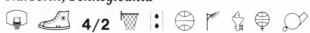 4/2

A gem of a court on Philly's Main Line. Old-timers (aged thirty to fifty) play weekends on the Tartan surface, while high-school-aged kids draw hundreds to courtside grandstands for summer league games.

6th Street Courts
6th and Boardwalk
Ocean City, New Jersey

 6/3

Jersey Shore hoop at its best, with aging Philadelphians like Matt Goukas and Bill Melchionni playing summer pick-up.

Virginia Avenue School Playground
Virginia
Petersburg, Virginia

 **6/4**

The bulrushes in which Moses Malone was found.

Maymount Elementary School
Allen and Amelia
Richmond, Virginia

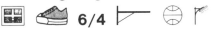 **2/1**

Bob Dandridge is one of the pros to come out of Maymount. Mostly full-court here; for half-court play, try the nearby Cary School courts.

Riis Park, Far Rockaway, New York

Candy Cane City
Rock Creek Park
Silver Spring, Maryland

 6/3

Be sure to bring quarters for the meter on the lights if you plan to play at night.

Cadwalader Playground
Parkside and West State
Trenton, New Jersey

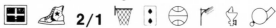 2/1

Spectators bet on games while digesting hot dogs—wrapped in cold rolls and washed down with warm sodas—from a nearby stand. Counsels a vet: "To get a game, yell 'nexts,' wait for a response, and adjust accordingly."

Suffolk Avenue Court
Suffolk and Boardwalk
Ventnor, New Jersey

 2/1

A half block away from the ocean, this is the former stomping ground for pro guard Chris Ford.

Princess Anne Park
Princess Anne and Landgston
Virginia Beach, Virginia

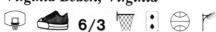 6/3

The word on the shore is that they run a ways inland, at Princess Anne in Virginia Beach proper.

Fort Stevens Park
13th and Van Buren N.W.
Washington, District of Columbia

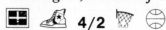 4/2

After shouting "I'm down" for the next game, scope out the sidelines for a familiar face—like Kenny Carr, Adrian Dantley, Larry Wright, or Kermit Washington—that might help.

Borsall Park
Silverside
Wilmington, Delaware

  2/1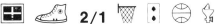

Proving ground for a bundle of Delaware All-Staters.

Metro Big Apple

It's undeniably the playground basketball capital of the world, and some of its best-known schoolyards are veritable open-air halls of fame. In Brooklyn, it's the Bed-Stuy, Bushwick, and Brownsville slabs, where you'll find the best outside-shooting street players in the city; in Harlem, parks filled with guys who do stuff under the basket that would get five to ten at Attica if done anywhere else; in Queens, the Rockaways, whose cottage industry is turning out white jump shooters; in the Village, artsy types who compose odes to their J's as they let them go. And though the quality of ball— along with the quality of just about everything else—is on the wane in the Bronx, other hoops outside the city proper but inside New York's magnetic field have risen to prominence. Some terrific "black" white players are coming out of Jersey City, just across the Hudson; "suburban" blacks have turned Mount Vernon and Rockville Centre into state high school powers, and the "Let's-switch-hoops-at-six-I-want-to-get-an-even-tan" crowd in the Hamptons suns itself on a tremendous beach-side court. Nets are hard to come by—especially within the Apple's core—but a satisfying, hard-nosed run isn't.

Foster Park
Foster and Nostrand
Flatbush, New York

You'll find everything from a Fly to a King at Foster, the celebrated heaven of playgrounds. When many are waiting to play, games go to twelve, straight. Best runs can be found on the court closest to the street; weekend afternoons are reserved for tourney action.

Jacob Riis Park
On-the-Beach
Far Rockaway, New York

New Yorkers symbolically begin and end the pick-up summer with pilgrimages to Riis Park over the long Memorial and Labor Day weekends. The salty breezes cool the court, but the sandy patches can make it treacherous.

West 4th Street Playground
West 4th and Sixth
Greenwich Village, New York

The crowd outside the fence—tourists, gays, and artsy types—is as motley a group as the roster of notables who have played here is impressive. Kareem Abdul-Jabbar, Tony Jackson, and Roger Brown have hacked and pushed in the lane at West 4th Street, known among Villagers as Death Valley.

Mimosa Beach Club
Dune
Hampton Bays, New York

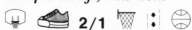

Just pulled a facial or blew a chippie? Celebrate by buying a round for your teammates, or drown your sorrows by yourself: There's a fully stocked bar right next to the court. Weekends see partying and ballplaying, ballplaying and partying.

West Fourth Street Playground, New York City

Holcombe Rucker Memorial Playground
155th and Eighth
Harlem, New York

"The Battleground" in Harlem, home of the Rucker Tournament, and an obligatory stop for any basketball fan. Unless you're All-World, or at least All-City, plan to watch, not play, and try to run down Robert, the P.A. announcer, for a dosage of Rucker lore.

St. Joseph's Schoolyard
511 Pavonia
Jersey City, New Jersey

Full-court only played here, the nation's leading proving ground for white, street-smart players. Surface is slightly inclined, so try to go downhill on offense. Loads of delis nearby.

Mt. Vernon Basketball Center
West 4th and Seventh
Mt. Vernon, New York

 6/2

The playground that bred Williamses Gus and Ray is run by the man who is the answer to the trivia question, "Who is the *brother* of the pitcher who gave up Bobby Thompson's play-off home run?"

Central Park
84th and Fifth
New York City, New York

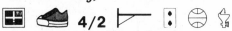 4/2

Very pleasant setting, though the elm tree branches can make corner jumpers problematic. Be sure to check out the Etruscan vases at the Metropolitan Museum, a few blocks away, between runs.

South Norwalk Playground
Woodward
Norwalk, Connecticut

 12/6

Calvin Murphy developed his wizardry here, where there are so many people waiting to play that all games are run "straight."

Scalzi Park
Bridge
Stamford, Connecticut

 2/1

On Mondays during the summer you can play to the sounds of a weekly outdoor music concert.

Breadbasket

Flatland and basketball were made for each other. There's a lot of solo played next to silos out here, with occasional bouts of barn-ball basketball in second-story haylofts. As a result, you'll find plenty of fine shooters, but a lot of odd shooting motions and bizarre trajectories, too. Keep in mind that you get what you earn out here, and nothing more: Score is always kept by ones.

WHERE IT'S AT

 Urban

 Suburban, Shorefront or Campus

 Small town or Rural

BEST COMP

 Occasional pro or Top-flight college

 Average college or Top-flight high school

 Average high school or Recreational Adult

 Junior high or Hacker

HOOPS AND SLABS

6/8 *Number of baskets/Number of full courts*

RACK AND TWINE

 Level rim with net

 Level rim without net

 Bent rim with net

 Bent rim without net

MISCELLANEOUS

 Games played according to "Deuce"

 Games played according to "Winner's Out"

 Court equipped with working lights

 Working drinking fountain nearby

 Women play often

 Organized summer league

Douglas Park
Providence
Columbia, Missouri

  12/4

The place to play in Columbia, and a hangout for many University of Missouri players.

Good Park
17th and University
Des Moines, Iowa

  4/2

Smack in the middle of downtown Des Moines. Corny it's not.

Myrtle Livingston Recreation Park
East Dunklin and Lafayette
Jefferson City, Missouri

 3/1

Urban renewal at its best. A half-court area is provided for warming up.

Malone Community Center
22nd and "T"
Lincoln, Nebraska

 2/1

Ask Dennis about the league he runs here, and hail any visiting Cornhuskers that happen by.

City Hall Court
8500 Sante Fe
Overland Park, Kansas

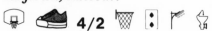 2/1

Games to fifteen and you gotta win by two.

Minor Smith Court
81st and Ash
Raytown, Missouri

 4/2

The action is always heavier here than on the nearby tennis courts. One of the few outdoor spots in the Kansas City area, where the gym is preferred to the playground.

Lanthier Park
Converse and Michigan
Springfield, Illinois

 4/2

With a street address like Converse and Michigan, you'll be playing on a court as American as the game itself.

WHERE IT'S AT

Emporia Street Park
North Emporia
Wichita, Kansas

 2/1

It's in a white neighborhood, but the players—including facial-administrator extraordinaire Darnell Valentine—are of a darker hue.

Tobacco Road

While you won't see players huddle after every basket, the influence of the Atlantic Coast Conference and its disciplined brand of ball is evident in games throughout North Carolina. When they run fast breaks, they do so methodically: ball to the middle and fill those lanes. The kids are passionate about the game and take it very seriously, while weekends see doctors, lawyers, and bankers opting for half-court hoop instead of golf or tennis. The facilities are fine, both indoors and out, thanks largely to North Carolina's activist recreation departments. And the state's mecca is Rocky Mount, that small city that produced Phil Ford, where they're putting up a network of seven spanking-new public gyms.

WHERE IT'S AT

 Urban

 Suburban, Shorefront or Campus

 Small town or Rural

BEST COMP

 Occasional pro or Top-flight college

 Average college or Top-flight high school

 Average high school or Recreational Adult

 Junior high or Hacker

HOOPS AND SLABS

6/8 Number of baskets/Number of full courts

RACK AND TWINE

 Level rim with net

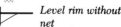 Level rim without net

 Bent rim with net

Bent rim without net

MISCELLANEOUS

 Games played according to "Deuce"

 Games played according to "Winner's Out"

 Court equipped with working lights

 Working drinking fountain nearby

 Women play often

 Organized summer league

Granville Towers Court
Franklin
Chapel Hill, North Carolina

 2/1

Mostly half-court, casually competitive games, though an occasional Dean Smith pupil takes part. Stereo and sunbathers nearby.

Freedom Park
Sterling and East
Charlotte, North Carolina

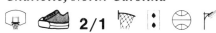 2/1

Not much to look at, but any court that claims Bobby Jones and Walter Davis as alums is worth noting.

Independence Park
7th and Park
Charlotte, North Carolina

 2/1

The games are played full court on weekdays and half court on the weekends.

Lyon Park
Lakewood
Durham, North Carolina

 4/2

Set amidst a grove of trees and next to a brook, the site of these two courts is as scenic as the moves of "Big Wheel" Rafton, a court regular, are freaky.

West Durham Recreation Center
Hillandale
Durham, North Carolina

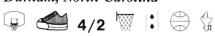 4/2

An affirmatively active playground in a pleasant setting. The crowd is on the elderly side and the action is generally on weekends.

OPPOSITE PAGE:
University of North Carolina's Granville Towers, Chapel Hill, North Carolina

Lake Daniel Park
East Lake
Greensboro, North Carolina

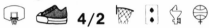 2/1

Richard Flinchum, a dentist who frequents the park, says he's looking for a house on this side of town so he can be near the court.

Carmichael Courts
Cater
Raleigh, North Carolina

 4/2

Going to the four corners is the quickest way to make enemies at these courts, on the North Carolina State University campus.

Buck Leonard Park
Grace and West End
Rocky Mount, North Carolina

 2/1

More hoop per capita than any other town in the state. Ballplayers vacate Buck Leonard by afternoon for indoor spots like the Booker T. and South Rocky Mount Rec Centers. Sunset Park claims the Sunday afternoon games, and girls run with the guys on Tuesday nights at Booker T.

Happy Hill Park
Alder
Winston-Salem, North Carolina

4/2

As popular as the games are here, the Wednesday night dances throughout the summer draw even bigger crowds.

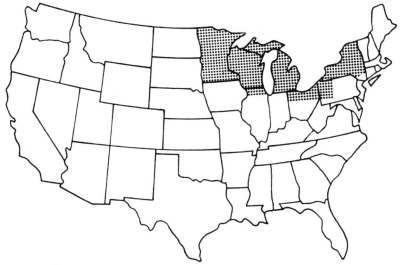

 Urban

 Suburban, Shorefront or Campus

 Small town or Rural

BEST COMP

 Occasional pro or Top-flight college

 Average college or Top-flight high school

 Average high school or Recreational Adult

 Junior high or Hacker

HOOPS AND SLABS

6/8 Number of baskets/Number of full courts

RACK AND TWINE

 Level rim with net

—— Level rim without net

Bent rim with net

Bent rim without net

MISCELLANEOUS

 Games played according to "Deuce"

 Games played according to "Winner's Out"

 Court equipped with working lights

Working drinking fountain nearby

 Women play often

 Organized summer league

Great Lakes

Long winters confine ballplayers to gyms in cities like Milwaukee (check out Franklin Square North), Chicago (Navy Pier in the North, Malcolm X Junior College in the South), and Detroit (Ceciliaville is really the St. Cecilia Church Gym, but they changed the name so people don't think they have to be Catholic to play there). Pick-up ball in the rim of cities along the lakes is governed by the standard urban trinity of conventions: (1) If people are waiting, games are "straight"; (2) You make it, you definitely take it; and (3) Being "down" don't mean nothin', as they say, if someone with a rep happens by.

Lion's Park
Silver Lake
Cuyahoga Falls, Ohio

 **4/2**

For the hardy, the town plows the courts off in the winter.

Valle Court Park
201 Hillside
East Lansing, Michigan

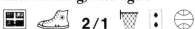 **2/1**

A small downtown park that draws well. Not unusual to find Michigan and Michigan State players in the games, including ex-Spartan "Magic" Johnson.

North Commons Community Rec Center
1800 James North
Minneapolis, Minnesota

The spawning ground of Ron Behagen and Archie Clark. When the weather's bad—as it so often is—there are six more hoops indoors.

Central Schoolyard
Niles Central Jr. High
Niles, Michigan

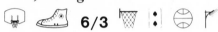

The nearby Dairy Queen offers the best in junk food for that post-game thirst and appetite.

East Hills Park
Wilmer
Pittsburgh, Pennsylvania

Weekday evenings during the summer, don't come to play, come to watch: The East Hills–Connie Hawkins Summer Basketball League may include the Hawk, Billy Knight, Norm Nixon, or Maurice Lucas.

Mellon Park
5th and Shady
Pittsburgh, Pennsylvania

The hoop here is more casual than at East Hills, though it's mostly full court. If you don't have a rep, or don't know anyone, be sure to get there right at 5:30, when the runs start.

Cobbs Hill Park
Monroe and Culver
Rochester, New York

Best players gravitate toward the court nearest the softball field. Watch for the metal knob which sticks up near half court, and can turn an opportunity for a fast break into one for a skinned knee.

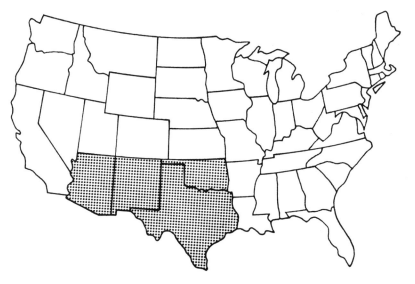

WHERE IT'S AT

 Urban

 Suburban, Shorefront or Campus

 Small town or Rural

BEST COMP

 Occasional pro or Top-flight college

 Average college or Top-flight high school

 Average high school or Recreational Adult

 Junior high or Hacker

HOOPS AND SLABS

6/8 Number of baskets/Number of full courts

RACK AND TWINE

 Level rim with net

 Level rim without net

 Bent rim with net

Bent rim without net

MISCELLANEOUS

 Games played according to "Deuce"

 Games played according to "Winner's Out"

 Court equipped with working lights

 Working drinking fountain nearby

 Women play often

Organized summer league

Sun Belt

The center of pick-up ball in the Southwest is Houston's Fonde Recreation Center. It's notorious throughout the state and—not by accident—it's an indoor facility; the air conditioning is great. Just make sure you're on supervisor Angelo Cascio's good side, since he decides who has "nexts." Until early evening the sun won't let you play outdoors in this region. And if you see immigration officials cruising parks in Chicano neighborhoods, it may be because they know that Mexican-Americans play half-court and illegal aliens run full.

Wells Park
5th and Mountain
Albuquerque, New Mexico

  6/3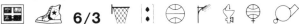

Plenty of present and former UNM Lobo players at these three courts, which are next to a gym. For the best facility in town, try Trumbull Park; for a rough game, Dennis Chavez Community Center; for a pleasant mix of students and locals, Heights Community Center.

Wooten Playground
Lazy and Dale
Austin, Texas

  4/1

The lights are great, the weather perfect.

Samuell Park
Garland
Dallas, Texas

 8/4

Mostly half-court play. You just might bump into Lee Trevino . . . not on the court, but on the nearby golf course.

Fred Moore Park
Lakely and Wilson
Denton, Texas

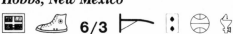 4/2

All games are played to twenty by twos.

Washington Park
4th and Gypsy
Hobbs, New Mexico

 6/3

A big-city brand of ball in an unlikely setting. Little Charlie Criss and ex-pro Bill Bridges are among the alumni, and local juco and high school talent keep the park at full capacity.

Memorial Park
N.W. 36th and Western
Oklahoma City, Oklahoma

 2/1

The only outdoor spot in town; most of the action is found at one of the eight municipal gyms.

Encanto Park
North 15th and Holly
Phoenix, Arizona

 2/1

Most heterogeneous run in Phoenix. Three-on-Three half-court is the most popular game. "Make it take it" is the rule, except among some whites in from the suburbs.

Wells Park, Albuquerque,
New Mexico

Hermosa Park
20th and Southern
Phoenix, Arizona

  2/1

Baddest runs in town. It isn't unusual to bump into a pro like Rudy White or Curtis Perry. Nothing but full-court, and don't forget to register on the sign-up board.

Carlos Gilbert Elementary School
Catron and Griffin
Sante Fe, New Mexico

   **2/1**

Pleasure City: All the rims are low, and you'll see lots of hackers fulfilling fantasies.

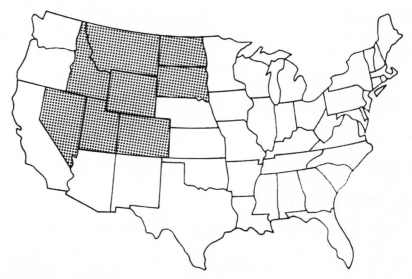

Big Sky—Rockies

A lot of rugged white players come out of the West, with Utah supplying more than its share. The style of ball out here is "white," too, and the games are short and sweet, usually to ten baskets. But if you're looking for a fix of inner-city run-and-gun, there are several possibilities. Two are on campuses: the E109 Gym at the University of Utah in Salt Lake City, and the University of Nevada–Las Vegas physical education building.

Optimist Park
Ryan and Hallwell
Billings, Montana

   4/2

One of four parks within Billings, each providing similar facilities. If there's no action here, cruise South, Lillis, and Rose Parks.

Holiday Park
16th and Morrie
Cheyenne, Wyoming

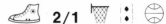   2/1

There's good comp here on weekdays, but at unpredictable times: The best athletes in town work for the railroads and oil refineries, and play hoop when their shifts are over.

Whittier Elementary School
28th and Bijou
Colorado Springs, Colorado

    2/1

Attracts a local, young, and not-too-high-powered clientele.

Farr Park
26th and Farr
Greeley, Colorado

  4/1

You'll find anything from hackers to collegians running here. A couple of side hoops.

Youth Center
201 Lead
Henderson, Nevada

  6/3

An orderly, civil game with no slam dunks and few arguments. Register on the chalkboard for winners, and be sure not to pick more then two players off the losing team.

Walter Johnson Memorial Park
East 3rd and Gray
Weiser, Idaho

2/0

Most games are played during the evening hours. It's all half-court.

Dixie

When below the Mason-Dixon line, look for a game during the late afternoon or twilight. The days are really too hot—especially in Florida—and many facilities come with lights. Also, if you're from out of town and score, don't immediately go backcourt and expect the ball back again: Odds are that they're playing losers' out, and you'll be branded a Yankee if you haven't already made it

WHERE IT'S AT

 Urban

 Suburban, Shorefront or Campus

 Small town or Rural

BEST COMP

 Occasional pro or Top-flight college

 Average college or Top-flight high school

 Average high school or Recreational Adult

 Junior high or Hacker

HOOPS AND SLABS

6/8 Number of baskets/Number of full courts

RACK AND TWINE

 Level rim with net

 Level rim without net

 Bent rim with net

 Bent rim without net

MISCELLANEOUS

 Games played according to "Deuce"

 Games played according to "Winner's Out"

 Court equipped with working lights

 Working drinking fountain nearby

 Women play often

Organized summer league

obvious by opening your mouth. For a pleasant, surprisingly high-quality run, check out the public courts in Florida beach resort cities like Fort Lauderdale and Daytona. College spring breaks during March and April drive the fabled pilgrims to the Atlantic shores, and they bring with them disparate playing styles. A lot of Bible Belt ball—in Atlanta, especially—takes place on churchyard courts, while cities like Memphis and Jackson, Mississippi, keep ballplaying confined largely indoors.

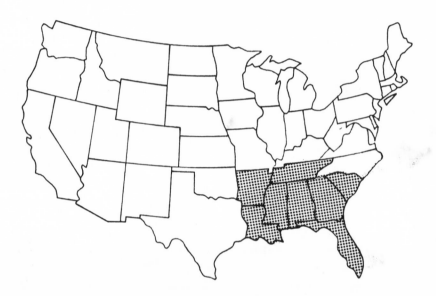

Seabreeze Recreation Center
Atlantic
Daytona Beach, Florida

 2/1

Off the main drag on the Daytona Beach strip, the perfect spot for stalking the on-court tan.

South Beach Picnic Area
Route A1A
Fort Lauderdale, Florida

 4/2

Right on the beach, and the place to mix it up with vacationing college students from all over. Rules vary because of variety of participants' backgrounds.

OPPOSITE PAGE:
Seabreeze Recreation Center, Daytona Beach, Florida

Jefferson Playground
Jefferson
Jacksonville, Florida

 12/2

Kids' Annex:  6/2

Two slabs here. A "Kids' Annex" teems with after-school activity. Ball is always checked on the side in half-court games. Holley's Bar-B-Q truck dispenses food and blasts soulful tunes through its mounted loudspeakers.

Simon Johnson Community Center
Royal and Moncrief
Jacksonville, Florida

 4/1

Unlike nearby Jefferson Playground the only Truck you'll find here is Mr. Leonard Robinson, who grew up on this court. Distaff action is found on two half-court slabs.

MacArthur Park
11th and MacAlmont
Little Rock, Arkansas

 2/1

Stars from Eddie Miles to Sidney Moncrief take this park's namesake's vow, and return.

Wright Street Park
Wright
Marietta, Georgia

 4/2

Games to twenty-fours by twos, and you gotta win by two.

Tamiami Regional Park
S.W. 24th
Miami, Florida

2/1

The lone outdoor court here is part of a huge park complex. Aside from the many ball fields, tennis courts, the swimming pool, and other facilities, there are two indoor hoop courts.

Napoleon Playground
Napoleon and Shakespeare
New Orleans, Louisiana

  2/1

Serious attitudes and (sometimes) Slick Watts can be found here, where most of the action is half-court. Some of the best runs in town are found at the refurbished Shakespeare Park.

Morris Court
Cord and J
Pensacola, Florida

  4/2

Saturday morning games are quite popular. Games go to thirty by twos.

Daffin Park
Victory and Waters
Savannah, Georgia

  2/1

Any spectators showing up here are probably coming to watch the AA Savannah Braves baseball team play, not the hoopers.

Irwin Park
Irwin and Crescent
Spartanburg, South Carolina

  2/1

The place to go, for ball or just hanging out. If someone says they just "ate your lunch," chances are your shot is blocked and your brown bag still untouched. Other action in Spartanburg at Cleveland Park and Dorman High School.

Bryce Field
University of Alabama
Tuscaloosa, Alabama

  4/2

Best place for outdoor hoop action in an otherwise gridiron-oriented community. Near fraternity row, but most of the animals keep off the courts.

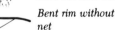

Northwest Kingdom

They love the game up here, but the weather doesn't. Fortunately it's just wet, not intemperate, and in their irrepressible way, northwesterners have fashioned covered but open-air courts. In Tacoma, they did it by building a slab under a highway overpass; in Eugene, by erecting a sheltering roof. Most action is half-court, to fifteen or twenty-one, by ones. So what if Perry Como lied about the bluest skies being in Seattle—the game plays on anyway.

Fish Creek Park
North Turnagin
Anchorage, Alaska

Evening games are best in midsummer, when there is daylight all night. Mostly half-court Three-on-Three. If there is no action, keep cruising: Every school in the city has an outdoor court.

Washington and Jefferson Street Park
First
Eugene, Oregon

Since some of the courts are covered, you needn't be a duck to play in wet weather. Lots of University of Oregon Ducks play anyway, though.

Fircrest Community Center
555 Contra Costa
Fircrest, Washington

   8/4

Enough courts here to keep everybody happy—nobody has to wait for a game.

Irving Park
N.E. 7th and Freemont
Portland, Oregon

     16/8

A mecca: Eight full courts, usually full on weekday evenings.

Liberty Park
1414 Houser
Renton, Washington

      2/1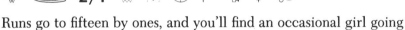

Runs go to fifteen by ones, and you'll find an occasional girl going with the guys.

Under-the-Freeway Courts
4th and McClellan
Spokane, Washington

     4/2

Keep your on-court chatter to a minimum, you're competing with the highway noise.

Sprinker Recreation Center
14824 South "C" Street
Tacoma, Washington

     8/4

These courts, located on a thirty-acre complex, provide a hangout for former Pac-10 officials, so the arguments are especially good.

WHERE IT'S AT

 Urban

 Suburban, Shorefront or Campus

 Small town or Rural

BEST COMP

 Occasional pro or Top-flight college

 Average college or Top-flight high school

 Average high school or Recreational Adult

 Junior high or Hacker

HOOPS AND SLABS

6/8 Number of baskets/Number of full courts

RACK AND TWINE

 Level rim with net

 Level rim without net

 Bent rim with net

 Bent rim without net

MISCELLANEOUS

 Games played according to "Deuce"

 Games played according to "Winner's Out"

 Court equipped with working lights

 Working drinking fountain nearby

Women play often

Organized summer league

WHERE IT'S AT

 Urban

 Suburban, Shorefront or Campus

 Small town or Rural

BEST COMP

 Occasional pro or Top-flight college

 Average college or Top-flight high school

 Average high school or Recreational Adult

 Junior high or Hacker

HOOPS AND SLABS

6/8 Number of baskets/Number of full courts

RACK AND TWINE

 Level rim with net

 Level rim without net

 Bent rim with net

 Bent rim without net

MISCELLANEOUS

 Games played according to "Deuce"

 Games played according to "Winner's Out"

 Court equipped with working lights

 Working drinking fountain nearby

Women play often

Organized summer league

Hill Country

It seems that there isn't a Kentucky town without a Dirt Bowl or Dust Bowl summer league, and each claims to have come up with the first one. But on this there's no argument: The basketball mania is equally intense throughout the region. In coal towns like Inez, Kentucky, and Bristol, Tennessee, life revolves around the high school team's fortunes, while in main cities like Charleston, West Virginia, participation is the thing—indoors in leagues at Oakes Field Gym, and outdoors, pick-up style, at Mound Park. Losers' out remains the rule in most of the area.

Central Elementary School Playground
Edgemont
Bristol, Tennessee

  **2/1**

A very small court, but popular enough to attract a fair-sized crowd at times. If no one is waiting, games are played to forty by ones.

City Park
Stadium
Bluefield, West Virginia

  **6/3**

Right near a nice picnic area. Someone can be found playing games to forty, by twos, almost anytime.

Pierce-Ford Tower Courts
Western Kentucky University
Bowling Green, Kentucky

  16/8

Other spots nearby: High Street Community Center (for run-and-gun) and Diddle Arena (when the team isn't practicing).

Schiller Park
City Park and East Deshler
Columbus, Ohio

  2/1

You needn't fear the comp here. Once a top spot, but the city's best are now doing their thing indoors.

Douglass Park, Lexington,
Kentucky

Inez Schoolyard, Inez, Kentucky

South Recreation Center
11th
Columbus, Ohio

   2/1

On the Ohio State University campus.

Inez Schoolyard
Route 40
Inez, Kentucky

   2/1

Coal country hoop at a great court, thanks to a now-deposed cage-loving county judge who had this facility installed. Ask anyone in Inez (pop. 450) about the local legends, the Stepp brothers.

Athletic Field
Lincoln
Latrobe, Pennsylvania

   4/2

An excellent summer league attracts loads of small-college players, and proves that a lot more than just Rolling Rock beer comes out of Latrobe.

Douglass Park
Georgetown and Howard
Lexington, Kentucky

  4/2

Also called the Skydome ("The only roof is the sky") or the Herb Washington Arena. Fantastic runs: If you can play, show your stuff to Melvin or Herb and they'll try to land you a scholarship. But if you just want to watch, check out a Dirt Bowl game and wash down Mother Green's cooking with some spirits from Booker T's drive-in liquor store, just across the street. The nets here must be replaced every two weeks.

Shawnee Park
Western and Market
Louisville, Kentucky

   8/4

The Dirt Bowl here is a Louisville landmark to match Churchill Downs. The ball is classic fast break, and a local says "even white folk come round once in a while." At tourney time, the tips in the food tent are just as good as the taps around the rim.

Kendall Perkins Park
West 5th
Owensboro, Kentucky

  4/2

Jerry, Dust Bowl director, says they run their small-town league with "big-town professionalism."

 WHERE IT'S AT

 Urban

 Suburban, Shorefront or Campus

 Small town or Rural

BEST COMP

 Occasional pro or Top-flight college

 Average college or Top-flight high school

 Average high school or Recreational Adult

 Junior high or Hacker

HOOPS AND SLABS
6/8 Number of baskets/Number of full courts

RACK AND TWINE

 Level rim with net

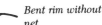 Level rim without net

 Bent rim with net

 Bent rim without net

MISCELLANEOUS

 Games played according to "Deuce"

 Games played according to "Winner's Out"

 Court equipped with working lights

 Working drinking fountain nearby

 Women play often

Organized summer league

Levinson-Pike Court
Levinson and Pike
Reading, Pennsylvania

Best runs are found on weekday evenings from six to ten P.M.

Clear Creek Park
7th
Shelbyville, Kentucky

Two brand-new courts nestled in the splendor of Kentucky blue-grass. Dan Issel's old spread is just a horseshoe toss away.

Golden Gate

California offers two sorts of venues: cityside or oceanside. In Los Angeles and San Diego, the best action is found indoors, in munici-pally maintained gyms. There aren't any hassles getting into them, the hours are liberal, and they're well supervised. San Diego's Mu-nicipal Gym, in lush Balboa Park, is a particularly alluring spot. Crowded Saturday mornings see the scoreboard clocks in use, put-ting a time limit on all half-court games, and local sports celebri-ties like baseball slugger Dave Winfield in intense games. Many of the public parks in Los Angeles County—like Normandie and Rogers—offer a choice between netless outdoor hoops and an indoor hall filled with activity. The beach communities in California—Laguna, Venice, Pacific, Mission—have well-kept outdoor slabs, usually near the surf, where the play is largely half-court. You can count on nets and, at some, an occasional pro. Far and away the best indoor comp in the North can be found in Cal-Berkeley's Harmon Gym; look for Golden State Warriors and their entourages of bountifully Afroed women and miscellaneous hangers-on.

Laguna Beach Playground
On-the-Beach
Laguna Beach, California

 **2/0**

Two beautiful half courts situated near golden-tressed sun worshipers and untressed Krishna worshipers. Three-on-Three is the most popular game, with weekend tournaments also a big hit. It takes twelve people to go Three-on-Three at Laguna: Six to go at each other on the court, and six more to share the experience.

Laguna Beach Playground, Laguna Beach, California (Rick Potter)

Denker Recreation Center
1550 West 35th
Los Angeles, California

 2/1

Once a prolific spot that turned out Guy Rodgers and Willie Naulls, the quality of comp has tailed off. Now almost a hackers' hangout.

Queen Anne Playground
Pico and Queen Anne
Los Angeles, California

 4/2

Laguna's summer Three-on-Three tourneys accommodate all ages and sizes. (Rick Potter)

A spicy ethnic flavor, and former stomping ground of Dick Barnett, Sidney Wicks, and Marques Johnson.

Venice Beach
On-the-Beach
Los Angeles, California

  4/2

Good chance to mix it up with UCLA, USC, and Laker players at a beautiful location, next to the crashing surf.

Bushrod Rec Center
59th and Shattuck
Oakland, California

  8/4

Funky ball in a funky setting, with an annual Easter Invitational Tourney that draws big crowds.

Tassafaronga Rec Center
85th and "G"
Oakland, California

  9/3

As many come for the action off the court as on; the ball is okay, but the music and dice games are better. Needless to say, everyone obeys Meminger's Law, "If you don't play ball, you can't hang out."

Fruitridge Community Park
Mendocino and Fruitridge
Sacramento, California

  2/1

A brand new facility. No established traditions as yet.

Funston Playground
Laguna and Bay
San Francisco, California

  2/1

Strictly half-court played here. A good ethnic mix on the weekends.

Stagg High School
1521 Brookside
Stockton, California

  6/2

Weekends find the courts deserted, while after school and weekday evenings the action picks up.

Hoosierland

Hoosiers really are hysterical about hoop, and the state is varied enough to include well-kept courts in cozy small towns (check out Martinsville, Richmond, and Springs Valley, as for instances) as well as teeming hubs of activity near its cities (though most courts in Indianapolis and Evansville can't seem to shirk that suburban wholesomeness). If you're a visitor, remember that, aside from being a bastion of Middle American folkways and attitudes, Indiana is one of the last refuges of losers' out.

Iglehart Park
First
Evansville, Indiana

  4/2

Best runs in the evening. Lots of setting up on offense, even in full-court games.

Kimball Park, Springs Valley, Indiana

Reservoir Park
Lafayette and Clinton
Fort Wayne, Indiana

   2/1

No, this isn't Iowa, but the girls playing here could hold their own there.

Ben Davis High School
10th and Girl's School
Indianapolis, Indiana

  8/4

Fine facility for integrated runs, with best comp claiming the court nearest the school. The Ponderosa Steak House on nearby 10th Street provides unlimited refills on soft drinks for that post-game thirst.

City Park
Home
Martinsville, Indiana

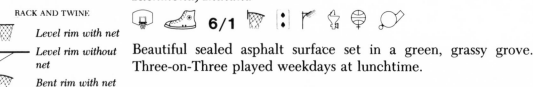 6/2

Quintessential Hoosier basketball . . . and why not? This is John Wooden's hometown. Loads of current and past high school players, all fundamentally sound.

McCulloch Park
Broadway
Muncie, Indiana

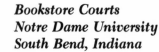 2/1

The pride they take in their state championship teams keeps the pick-up spirit running high.

Clear Creek Park
Route 40 and S.W. 11th
Richmond, Indiana

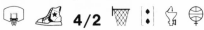 6/1

Beautiful sealed asphalt surface set in a green, grassy grove. Three-on-Three played weekdays at lunchtime.

Bookstore Courts
Notre Dame University
South Bend, Indiana

4/2

Site of the fabled Notre Dame Bookstore Basketball Tournament every April. Beware the manhole cover at mid-court.

Meadowood Park
Meadowood and Parkwood
Speedway, Indiana

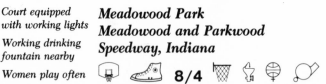 8/4

Located in a white suburban neighborhood, but blacks come anyway. As a result, there's some latent racial tension, but nothing serious. Watch the overhanging tree branches on your J from the corner.

Kimball Park
Route 56
Springs Valley, Indiana

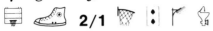

Where locals crow about Larry Bird, who perfected his turn-around fadeaway "J" here, and whose apprenticeship is commemorated by a sign.

About the Authors

CHUCK WIELGUS, JR., thirty, is Director of Recreation in Woodstock, Vermont. A graduate of Providence College, he received his master's degree from Springfield College in 1974 and has since coached basketball at the high school and college levels. He and his wife, Christina, women's basketball coach at Dartmouth College, have a year-old son, Chip, who has already bent several training rims. Chuck beats Alex at H-O-R-S-E.

ALEXANDER WOLFF, twenty-three, has studied history at Princeton University and written for *The New York Times, Time,* and Reuters. While playing basketball for a year in Lucerne, Switzerland, he contributed to international understanding by explaining to teammates what a *Gesichtarbeit* (face job) is. Alex beats Chuck at Around-the-World.